Advanced Praise for
ADOPTING GRACE

This is an accessible yet profound spiritual autobiography. In her search for God's preferred future for her biological and adopted children, Tricia Wilson discovers God's preferred future for herself. In seeking abundant life for her family she enters into abundant life of her own.   She manages a rare feat – sharing her wounds without picking personal scabs. Her unabashed candor with regard to her personal challenges is a model of how we all ought to live. The literary references are varied and engaging and the resource guide at the end is comprehensive and proven. I recommend this to any who seek to know more fully about the loving and gracious God of us all.

> ~Rev. Bruce E. Stanley, President/CEO, Methodist Home for Children

Tricia Wilson, an honest storyteller, invites the reader to travel with her on a "real life" journey toward soul freedom. She demonstrates courage in building relationships, asking forgiveness, and learning for life. The book brought tears to my eyes and hope for my spirit. I highly recommend embarking on a spiritual journey with this writer.

> ~Ka'thy Gore Chappell, Leadership Development Coordinator, Cooperative Baptist
> Fellowship of North Carolina

Tricia Wilson has provided a compelling travelogue for all who feel stuck in the journey we call parenthood. We are invited to walk alongside the author as she learns to walk alongside her children. Wilson unpacks the bag of tools that helped her in her spiritual, emotional, and thoughtful journey.

> ~David Smoot, Ph.D, Child and Family Psychologist, Raleigh, NC

This is a great read for anyone on the path towards self-actualization. Especially if you are a parent with a calling to find your best self and/or seeking to open your heart and let love in! Wilson courageously shares her journey through perhaps some of the most difficult issues we can face. Not only does she look at who she was as a Mother but begins to dissect the religious belief systems and culture that formed who she had become in this role.

> ~Helene Timpone, LCSW

There's a vulnerable, and in my opinion, a very refreshing quality about Wilson's writing. In a culture where people/parents often struggle to lay themselves bare, *Adopting Grace* will help its readers explore opportunities to live more honestly and with grace.
I had a moment when Wilson's narration of shame touched me to the point of tears. This isn't a read where you'll simply be consuming loads of information. You will feel. You will connect. You will have a moment.

> ~Reverend Lisa Yebuah, Campus Pastor, SERT of Edenton Street UMC

Adopting Grace

ADOPTING GRACE

A Parenting Journey from Fear to Freedom

by

Tricia Wilson

library partners press
a digital publishing imprint

First Edition

ISBN: 978-1-61846-041-7

Scripture quotations marked NLT are taken from the Holy Bible, New Living Translation, copyright ©1996, 2004, 2007, 2013, 2015 by Tyndale House Foundation. Used by permission of Tyndale House Publishers, Inc., Carol Stream, Illinois 60188.

Scripture quotations marked MSG are taken from THE MESSAGE, copyright © 1993, 1994, 1995, 1996, 2000, 2001, 2002 by Eugene H. Peterson. Used by permission of NavPress.. Represented by Tyndale House Publishers, Inc.

Scripture quotations marked NRSV are taken from New Revised Standard Version Bible, copyright © 1989 National Council of the Churches of Christ in the United States of America. Used by permission.

All Scripture quotations, unless otherwise indicated, are taken from the Holy Bible, New International Version®, NIV®. Copyright ©1973, 1978, 1984, 2011 by Biblica, Inc.™ Used by permission of Zondervan.. The "NIV" and "New International Version" are trademarks registered in the United States Patent and Trademark Office by Biblica, Inc.™

The artwork on the cover was created by Rose Lynne Clinkscales Bowman of Winston-Salem, NC. "Tricia's Midway Journey" was commissioned and a gift from the author's husband on the occasion of her 53rd birthday. The cover design and interior flourishes were created by the author's son, Chris Younkin-Wilson of Chicago, IL.

The author has recreated events, locales and conversations from memory. In order to maintain anonymity in some instances, names of individuals and places, and some identifying characteristics and details such as physical properties, occupations and places of residence may have been changed.

Library Partners Press
ZSR Library
Wake Forest University
1834 Wake Forest Road
Winston-Salem, North Carolina 27106

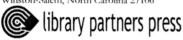 library partners press

a digital publishing imprint

www.librarypartnerspress.org
Manufactured in the United States of America

To my children,

you are the grace bearers in my life.

CONTENTS

INTRODUCTION

I married quite young for a college educated woman. Exactly two months post-graduation and at the age of 21, I walked down the aisle. The man I fell in love with is an ambitious man. Psychologists say that we often marry those that feel like "home," and this was my comfortable dwelling place. While he was making his way up in the corporate world, I was doing the same in my mom and volunteer life. Even before we married, we agreed on three children. My husband Mark verbalized his desire to have these children by the time he was thirty years old so that we could be young and free empty nesters– this goal was just narrowly missed as our third son entered the world a mere three days after Mark's 30th birthday. It all appeared very nice and tidy and American dreamish.

As our sons got older and this mama wasn't quite ready to retire from my job and the identity it provided, my internal adoption heartbeat picked up the pace. Through the years, we have often been asked the question, "Why did you adopt?" After a lot of therapy and mindfulness and meditation before God, I now respond, "Do you want the practical, emotional, or spiritual answer to that question?"

Practical—I wasn't ready to give up and retire from the main career path I had followed. The demands of my husband's chosen occupation were high and being mom was something that I enjoyed and could mesh with his job.

Emotional—There were things from my own childhood and life that needed attention and working out. Because I am a female, parenting daughters was a more direct path to doing so.

Spiritual—While waiting for our first daughter to come into our family, a friend said these words to me: "This adoption is more about God changing you than it is about changing the lives of the children who will enter your family." Amen to that.

I think that we often spiritualize the practical and emotional and then just as easily offer practical or emotional explanation for that which is spiritual. It seems to me that they all come bound up and intertwined as we travel this planet.

Within a group of Christian adoptive parents, there is a savior mentality when bringing an orphaned child into our midst. God forgive me, I had more of that inside of me than I care to admit or dwell on at this stage of life. People aren't saviors and the realities and powers at work are so much more nuanced, complex, confusing, and full of joy and pain.

Yet I do believe that despite the ways we veer off, twist, turn, and justify our behaviors and choices, this proverb is always in motion, "Many are the plans in a person's heart, but it is the Lord's purpose that prevails."[1] Despite my own self and lack of awareness, God is at work.

After adopting our daughters, somewhere along a three-year fog of sleep deprivation, night terrors, and behavioral challenges, I as mother came to a critical crossroad. There was a big rage and tantrum that went on for hours. I pulled out all of the tools in my parenting toolbox, got to the bottom, and it was completely empty. It was as if in that moment, God bent down and whispered, or more accurately yelled, into my ear, "You can change yourself and your parenting or you can dig in, cling to your old ways, and in the process destroy two children. This is your choice." That was holy ground. It was a sacred invitation to a step-by-step journey.

I remember a showdown in our home between my then CEO husband and our then preschool aged daughter. Highly paraphrased, this exasperated dad said, "I am in charge of a large company and people do what I say. But I can in no way control this twenty-pound little girl." Thanks be to God for the things in life over which we have no control. They are so very often the vehicles of grace moving into our lives. This book chronicles the lessons learned along my motherhood journey toward adopting grace for myself, my family, and others.

CHAPTER 1

○

REPEATER DAYS

*"Wont to unlearn from history,
we aptly repeat even its most brazen mistakes."*
Eskinder Nega

I have heard it said that those of us who become parents choose one of three pathways. We repeat the parenting practice of our own parents. We totally rebel against the way in which we were raised. Or healthiest of all, we intentionally consider what we desire to keep from our parents' ways and what we want to change. The path chosen informs values taught, faith expression passed along, and hundreds of daily decisions that affect our children. Unless we choose the third pathway, we mostly roll along living, as well as parenting, from an unconscious place. As I entered into the early days of being a mom, I was most often a repeater.

I find this interesting. Raised in a conservative Southern Baptist church, I have been on a lifetime journey to make peace with myself, the Christian faith, and with God. Many doubts and questions about this particular brand of religion were present and rolling around my heart and mind from a very young age. But it took time and courage to put the misgivings on the table and carefully examine them.

For much of my life, matters of faith and following God felt like a chore or some kind of cruel cosmic exam. It felt like an exercise in stumbling through an intentionally difficult maze, taking a test while desperately seeking all of the right answers, or tripping through a war zone trying to avoid hidden land mines. My soul cried out for something different.

The atmosphere in which my religious life was formed was legalistic. As a child, I had no awareness or vocabulary for such ideas. A fear of hell and damnation outmuscled any message of mercy or grace in my tenderhearted soul. Performance and image seemed to matter infinitely more than the truth and reality of what I witnessed around as well as inside of me. I did not know where to go to express the uncertainties that darted around my mind.

Up on the wall in my childhood bedroom, a nine by twelve framed print of a little girl kneeling in prayer while looking toward an ethereal light above was displayed. This mystical glow somehow satisfied my young soul. Is that what God is like? I hope so. But the weekly Sunday message that always led to an invitation to step out of a place of damnation and into one of salvation created great anxiety and fear within my impressionable heart. I walked that aisle a few different times hoping to satisfy the very hard to please God of my active and fearful imagination.

As I grew, the doubts, confusion, and questions continued. I remember as a teen going to leaders in my church and asking questions about the confusing messages I read in the Bible. The violence of God in the Old Testament, the contradicting ideas, and all those people who didn't believe like us destined for hell. It's a really big world out there, you know? The dismissal of my questions, non-answers, and admonitions to just have "faith" were totally unsatisfying. Were these leaders afraid of such questions?

I enjoyed several close friendships with peers in my church. We had a lot of fun on mission trips. I saw the lives of others up close and fell in love with a little boy that I taught in Vacation Bible School in the Bronx. I smoked my first and only cigarette, played a few games of spin the bottle, and felt a bit of freedom, but mostly guilt, while doing so. I laughed a lot with my fellow youth group friends on these trips and sometimes enjoyed our twice weekly gatherings. I got to sing in choirs, and that often made me feel happy. There were a few Sunday School teachers and one minister of music that I truly loved. They modeled grace.

But it was also very confusing. At one particular youth retreat, the explicit teaching was to have a closed mind. I can still remember the visual props that had bright yellow warning road signs with the precise message "open minds-closed for repairs." Having an open mind as we headed toward higher education and beyond was discouraged and warned against. Fear overpowered any messages of grace.

When I was in college, a youth minister from my childhood church told me that God had told him that I was going to be a minister's wife and what an amazing privilege and special call that would be. At that point in my life, I was pretty sure I was going to be Mark's wife, and minister did not seem to be his calling. Though I could not give clear voice to the idea at the time, an internal discomfort around the differing male and female roles and privileges within this religious tradition was budding. My evolving feminist sensibilities within whispered that "wife of minister" may not always be such a great gig.

During three and a half years of dating, Mark and I talked of our expectations and vision of marriage and family. We both hailed from fairly traditional and conservative homes, and we envisioned that we would follow suit. He wanted to pursue a career, and my wishes were, if possible, to stay home and focus my energy on raising children. That had always been my dream.

As a teen and young adult, I had an unusual habit whenever I was in a department store. I enjoyed going to the baby shoes section and internally oohing and ahhing over the amazingly adorable mini sandals, moccasins, and tiny little dress up shoes. I babysat some, but my favorite times were when all the children were asleep, and I could just look at the toys and baby stuff and dream of my own future children. Sometimes, these imaginary children were adopted children.

As I traveled away from my growing up home and toward a small liberal arts university, one that was in the midst of breaking ties with the religious denomination of my youth, I was anxious and thrilled at the same time. My parents gave me great voice and choice in this decision even though I imagined that deep down they were a little, or maybe a lot, afraid of what I might learn there. A few adults in my world warned me of the dangers of a liberal education.

I quickly connected with a Christian fellowship on campus and began to find my places and spaces in this new home. I avoided most of the fraternity parties because of the teetotal religious teaching of my church. In time, I got involved in a church and joined a campus sorority so that I could be a good influence on the "heathens."

At one point, in order to participate in leadership, the adult leader of my college fellowship group called a meeting and required all of us to sign an agreement to "The Chicago Statement on Biblical Inerrancy."[2] Inerrancy was a buzzword being thrown around the world of evangelical Christianity during this time. This 1978 statement created by a group of conservative evangelical leaders addresses the authority of scripture and was written in response to their perceived threat of liberal theology. It was a type of litmus test to mark the "true believers."

I was already a bit suspicious of this fellowship leader, because a female friend of mine who was slated to be the next president of our Christian organization had been asked to step aside due to her gender. This was uncomfortable for me, but not a new concept since my own childhood church did not and still does not allow women to hold most leadership roles. I can't remember if I signed the statement, but I am afraid I did. I was a small group leader for a few years, and I am pretty sure that would not have been allowed if I hadn't put my signature on that piece of paper.

At the same time, I moved down a path that became a pursuit and passion for years to come. I began taking psychology and religion classes, and to this day, I am working to integrate these two disciplines into a healthy pursuit of living. In religion classes, I was exposed to different ideas about the Bible, how it was written and formed, and a putting on the table of all things problematic to my inquisitive mind. I learned I wasn't the only one with faith questions and a desire to pursue answers with both head and heart. In psychology courses, I was introduced to new ideas around human thought, emotion, and behavior. These concepts were not emphasized in my family of origin.

This was an invigorating pursuit, yet it bumped up against so much that I was taught as a child. The tapes of my childhood discipline and religion blared inside my mind. Fear would often lead to panic and then to a shutdown of just how open minded and questioning I was willing to be. But it was a beginning, a crack in my confused and fearful mindset.

ﾟ○○○ﾟ

When I was twenty-seven years old, Mark and I and our two sons moved back to the place I grew up, and after looking into alternative worship places, we headed back to the church I spent much time in as a child. This led to a conflict for me. The life of peace and freedom that I heard talk of and that I so desired was not realized for me in this particular place of worship, and yet I returned there. We often gravitate to what we know, even when deep down we long for something different.

We spent two years living in this place before moving away. During a Bible study on Galatians in this church, a teacher shared a striking visual. It has come to mind over and over in subsequent years. I clearly remember him saying, "Following God is not something we have to figure out step by step. It is like running through a field." A vision of myself running through a grassy, flower filled place with hair flowing in the wind came to mind. This was radically different than the messages I had absorbed around relationship with the divine and "God's will." I had taken to heart a relationship that was full of striving and effort on my part coupled with a fear that any misstep would lead to a holy zap from above. "Like running through a field" offered a stark contrast, and this idea pricked a hopeful possibility. I glimpsed the prospect of freedom, joy, and fulfillment as this word picture captured my imagination. A vision of a God who laughed and delighted in me while I ran through this field with abandon was painted. Such a connection with God seemed so elusive to me, yet it was quite seductive. *That* was the kind of faith experience my heart desired.

This grace-laden perspective created a small opening within my heart. Maybe there was another way to experience faith and do life. I don't have to be a repeater. Though there would be many years and much hard work required before significant shift happened, this was a starting point. "Like running through a field" often whispered to my parched soul and offered hope as I sought to make peace within and without.

There is an Old Testament oft repeated message that falls in the category of "I really wish the Bible didn't say that." It goes like this: "The Lord is slow to anger, and abounding in steadfast love, forgiving iniquity and transgression, but by no means clearing the guilty, visiting the iniquity of the parents upon the children to the third and the fourth generation." (Numbers 14:18, NRSV)

It is the very last phrase that causes discomfort. Those who know Hebrew or Greek say that English often doesn't give justice to many biblical words. The meanings are often richer, more nuanced, than our language can convey. Iniquity is sometimes translated as sin or transgression, visiting as punishing, and on and on go the translation debates. But no matter the translation, the sentiment of this verse is disturbing and triggers my American sense of individuality and fairness.

I remember a conversation with a family member who had recently read all the way through the Bible. This particular repeating message of the sins of the parent being visited upon the children upset her, and she asked me what I thought. The only thing I could come up with was that it seemed realistic, yet I hoped it was not fatalistic.

It is true that without significant intervention, we as parents will repeat the dysfunction of our own parents who are just repeating that of their own parents, and thus it is transferred from generation to generation to generation. I remember learning that sometimes the word sin or iniquity is more accurately rendered "missing the mark," as in archery. Often rather than a willful choice or blatant wrong, our misdeeds are simply a repeating of what we have been taught or role modeled. It is quite an efficient system. We are bestowed both functional and dysfunctional mindset and behaviors by those who came before us. I am no exception.

The early days of being a new mom were filled with anticipation and excitement. My dream was coming true. I was just shy of twenty-five years old and naïve about the journey ahead. Who fully understands what we are signing up for when we enter parenthood? In the span of five years, three beautiful boys joined our family.

Espoused by leaders such as James Dobson, the conservative Christian parenting message of the day made a formulaic a+ b = c promise to those who followed a certain set of "biblical" teachings on how to be a successful parent. Dobson's voice was joined by others, and each proclaimed *the way* of Christian parenting. One such book was even titled *"Growing Kids God's Way."*[3] There were sometimes radio shows to go along with these ideas. I read a few such books and tuned in to the shows every once in a while. The proclaimed parenting paradigm was one that demanded respect and obedience with an emphasis on controlling a child's behavior, along with periodic spanking thrown in for good measure. I believed that to be a "good Christian mom," this was the path to follow.

Despite an internal disquiet around some of these parenting teachings, a deep fear of going against the status quo kept me "in line." What if I did things differently, and my children didn't "turn out" well? People in my world were watching me, and I wanted their approval. Fear held the reins of my parenting methods.

I was spanked, therefore I spanked. I remember long days with a two year old and newborn baby. Sometimes I held the baby to my breast with one hand and a spanking stick in the other. Of course, my toddler's world had been rocked with the entrance of a brother, but I bought into the idea that the only way to address misbehavior was to make him comply with the "rod of correction." Somehow one small Bible verse about sparing a rod and spoiling a child had led to justification for corporal punishment. Even though I was not a fan of the rod of correction in my own childhood, I still repeated. Conservative Christian books and messages provided support and rationalization for such choices.

Years later when my boys were teenagers, I stood in our kitchen chatting with my friend Susan. Susan is a mother to adopted children similar in age to our daughters. One of my then teenage sons walked in and joined in the conversation. The topic was discipline methods, and the subject of spanking arose. By this time I was a "reformed" spanker, and I imagine that gave my son permission to be honest about his experiences. He said these words: "I remember that whenever I got spanked, I felt humiliated." My heart dropped. I felt sad and embarrassed. Even though I no longer practiced corporal punishment, I regretted that I had ever done so. Humiliation of my child was never my conscious intent. Because I had not seen emotional connection modeled in a healthy way, I did not know how to come alongside my son when he was in emotional distress, and I sometimes defaulted to physical punishment. This practice certainly broke bonds and interfered with our mother-son relationship.

Why had I repeated a parenting practice that I myself hated when it had been applied to me as a child? I remember feeling helpless and then a furious anger when I was the recipient of corporal punishment. The only answer to my why question is that it requires a great deal of self-awareness and intention to change such patterns. My son's honest words on that day held up a mirror and gave me a chance to see myself more clearly.

Recently, I visited with my friend Beth who lived with our family one summer while she was in college. In exchange for room and board, she occasionally cared for our young sons so that Mark and I could go out and spend time together. As Beth and I sat on the couch, catching up on each other's lives, she said these words to me. "I am afraid that I messed up your son." Curious about what she was referring to, I asked her to explain. She recounted that one of our boys, around three years old at the time, was often particularly whiny and emotional. "He would get all whiny, I would send him to his room and set the microwave timer. He couldn't come out until he settled down." Then she said something very profound. "He was just expressing his feelings." My honest and a bit shame producing response was, "Who do you think told you to set that microwave timer?" Of course, I had.

As I recall scenes such as these, I sometimes feel embarrassed. Hindsight and greater knowledge about child development and emotional expression now offer a very different perspective. But like most mothers, I was doing the best I could at that time. My education about and acceptance of the vast world of feelings was not to come until years down the road. I was unintentionally passing along to my sons less than functional ways to deal with the powerful and sometimes overwhelming emotions of being human. In my younger mom years, "just make it stop" was the goal during any tantrum or heightened emotional expression. Particularly in the midst of one I deemed as "negative" emotion.

One of our sons struggled with anxiety that affected his daily life and led us to seek professional help when he was in the third grade. This was during a time when I was in deep denial around my own struggles with anxiety. I possessed no conscious vocabulary or awareness for the unhealthy coping mechanisms I had developed over many years.

I was in distress over the situation with our son and voiced out loud to my husband, "I feel adequate to deal with physical challenges, but not emotional ones. I don't like that our family is in need of this kind of help." Despite being a psychology major, the idea of a mind and body connection was foreign to me. Mark wisely replied, "We don't get to choose." During my boy's first appointment with the counselor, I cried and cried. Somewhere along the way I internalized a false belief that reaching out for help in the area of mental and emotional health is a type of weakness or failure. How misguided I was. The truth is that getting help was a huge relief. We needed it. Things were happening that we didn't have the tools to address, and our children and family would suffer if I let my pride stand in the way of reaching out for assistance.

The therapist who helped our son once gently brought up to me my own role in our family dynamic, but I wasn't ready to hear or accept this reality. It would come, but not yet. This counselor asked me if I made it a point to offer praise and encouragement to my boy. The honest answer was "rarely." Despite an overall discomfort with Dr. James Dobson's parenting advice, one helpful idea that I heard from him is that for every negative or corrective interaction we have with our children, we should have five positive or encouraging exchanges. I was extremely out of balance on this scale. Many of the mother and son exchanges in our home were corrective or critical. It took a conscious effort for me to listen to the words flying out of my mouth toward the tender hearts in my care to see this imbalance. I began to take baby steps toward a healthier balance.

I continued to read authors that agreed with and defended the conservative Christian parenting paradigm until one day I read a book called "Grace Based Parenting."[4] There was something deep in my soul that resonated with this text. On completion of that particular book and well into the task of raising three boys, I resolved to take a hiatus from reading about parenting and striving to get it "right." I needed to impart more grace to myself, to my children, and to others.

In many ways, I was a parenting repeater. Yet my mothering style was conjoined with a lot of internal rebellion against the religious teaching of my youth. I stoked an inner fire with misdirected anger toward my own parents. As I began to experience and consider the complexities and difficulties of being a mom, kindness toward myself and my parents crept into my heart. Just like me, they were doing the best that they knew how given the life they had lived. But at this point in life, I still was not courageous enough to go against much that I had been taught and seen modeled. I did not yet trust my gut or my own voice. Conservative religion had done a good job of instilling guilt and anxiety in me.

As parents, the choices we make do affect our children. The recurring message in the Old Testament about the iniquity of the parents being visited upon the children is realistic. Yet I also know that if there are things we desire to do differently and change within our own nuclear families, this can happen.

Rather than repeat or rebel, there is a third way. We can mindfully choose to carry forward those things that we value from our own childhood and at the same time make shifts around the things we want to shed. Very often, the impetus for such a change is the entrance of something dramatic and oft times painful into our lives. For me, this was just around the corner.

Reflection

Dear sons of mine,

I stand with Kierkegaard in this sentiment: "Life can only be understood backwards; but it must be lived forwards." There was much that your young mom had little understanding of as she joyfully welcomed you into this world. Though acknowledgement of this truth is critical, the deeper regret softens as time passes and forgiveness is extended. All that has come before today informs and revamps the relationship of this day as we walk hand in hand with grace alongside.

My wish for you is that with mindfulness and intention, you will shed repeating and rebelling, and choose your own way forward. It is with great love and respect that I stand on the sidelines and cheer you on as you create your very own story.

Love,
Mom

CHAPTER 2

○○

THE GAME CHANGER

Yet it is only love which sets us free.
Maya Angelou

A s I approached the age of forty, empty nest life was on the horizon. This appealed to my husband, but not to me. I had structured so much of my energy and identity around the role of mother as well as school and church volunteer. Since the possibility of adoption simmered just below the surface of my heart, this seemed like a good time to start dropping hints and pursuing conversation with Mark. We went to a meeting to learn more about becoming foster parents, but I didn't feel emotionally prepared for the ups and downs of that particular journey.

During this time period, in the early 2000's, many US evangelical leaders began to issue a call – a call to adoption. A number of high profile religious leaders and entertainers either adopted children themselves or joined the swelling voice and call for Christians to adopt orphans. Adoption became almost contagious within this group. Laced with messages of saving children and Christian duty, it appealed to a variety of people, some with a savior complex. There was often a romantic and beautiful veneer brushed across this call. I joined the ranks.

We started down the road toward adoption, and for both pragmatic and unconscious at the time reasons, we settled on adopting from China. Our sons were ostensibly on board, though how in the world can pre-teen and teenage boys have any idea what they are agreeing to when their parents are fairly clueless on the matter? At this point in time, our parenting journey with our sons rolled along with the mostly typical bumps in the road. People within our circles admired our family as they looked on from the outside. I brazenly and naively felt fairly prepared, adequate, and up to the task of adoption. I had this parenting thing down.

Though our adoption agency responsibly educated and challenged us to accept that parenting children who have experienced early relational trauma requires a special set of skills, I still wasn't so sure about that. "Love is enough" is a very common misconception for adoptive parents – well, that and the parenting skills I already possessed. During a home study visit, Mark and I both communicated that we were mostly comfortable with the way we were raising our sons, but we nodded assent to the possible need for change. Residing in a place of naiveté and pride, I had no idea what was ahead.

Quite irresponsibly and arrogantly, we adopted two toddlers within thirteen months of each other, including one child who had significant medical needs. I have since heard an expert in "children from hard places," Dr. Karyn Purvis, say that best outcome practice in the world of adoption is to adopt one at a time and at least three years apart.[5] Good advice.

Soon after we adopted our first daughter, discussions about adopting a second child popped up. For a variety of reasons, we hoped to adopt another child. Mark, who is very good at math, was concerned about our current projected age for the now distant empty nest days. Forty-two plus eighteen equals sixty. I had some kind of supermom complex. We were both in a hurry.

Any child that spends time in an orphanage or foster care comes into family with complex emotional needs. Our first daughter was no exception, but her temperament along with my unacknowledged deficits as mom allowed me to overlook some of her particular needs. Aside from sleep issues, her approach to the world did not interfere with my comfortable modus operandi of parenting. We forged ahead.

Though China matched us with a child the first time, we were more comfortable with the idea of adopting a child with medical needs on the second go round. There was a beautiful, big brown-eyed toddler that came to our attention. A non-profit called Love Without Boundaries provided an early surgery for this child, and several of their volunteers had met and interacted with her. One desired to adopt her, but her home country of Ireland would not allow it. The volunteers wrote passionately of this girl and described her as full of life and spunk, with a twinkle in her eye. "She sounds like the perfect girl for our family" said one of the big brothers. And indeed she was.

Our oldest son often says something like this, "When my younger sister entered our family, that was the game changer." He has two sisters who are temperamentally about as different as humanly possible. When it comes to our two daughters, they are opposite in more ways than one: Introvert vs extrovert, quiet vs loud, logical vs emotional, and the list could go on and on and on. In any family, some personalities blend in and "fit" our expectations, and there are others that create friction and rub against us. Sometimes the friction happens because a child is so very much like us, but we don't want to acknowledge that. Growth and change rise up in the midst of friction.

Our youngest child often refers to herself as "the grand finale." Before she entered our family, there were less than functional dynamics in play, but I was not particularly aware of these or my role in them. No person or situation had yet made me uncomfortable enough to consider another way. I wasn't ready to change. I believe that God is active even in the midst of our arrogance and ignorance. The grand finale was just what I needed to learn much about life and grace and myself.

After our daughters joined our family, I rapidly came up empty handed as I searched for parenting tools to address their particular needs. I had nothing. The conservative Christian formulas and advice not only didn't work, they made things worse. I needed a radical parenting shift.

It is a well-documented phenomenon that human beings will not change unless there is an overwhelming impetus kicking us in the pants. For many of us, only deep and profound pain provides enough motivation. Pain and failure as a mom was a grace disguised that entered my life with a bang and in both rough and gentle ways beckoned me to pursue ways of health and healing. Backed into a corner and falling apart, I had little choice but to listen and then respond.

Reflection

Dear daughters of mine,

As I drive around town, I often come up on bumpers sporting these words, "Who saved who?" Though meant to give honor to animals rescued, I always think of you when I read these words.

Though your earliest days were difficult, I admire your spirit and inner strength and courage. You amaze me. It is a gift and honor to stop, listen, and receive your voice as you call me mom.

As a mom sorely unprepared for the early days we shared together, thank you for being my teachers, my mentors, my salvation. You saved me from dogmatism and pride and being a know-it-all. You gently, and at times firmly, grabbed my hand and pulled me into a place of grace. Grace for myself, for each of my children, and for those I previously deemed "other."

Thank you for showing me that my call is not to save, but to walk alongside and embrace the full range of life together with you, my children. I hope that you always know that you are deeply and dearly loved.

Love,
Mom

CHAPTER 3

BECOMING FULLY HUMAN

Can true humility and compassion exist in our words and in our eyes
unless we know we too are capable of any act?
St. Francis of Assisi[6]

O ne message that I digested from the religion of my youth was that those of our particular "in crowd" were somehow different, set apart, and on the moral high ground. There was great emphasis on those who are "in" and those who are "out." It was a dogmatic world, and our people were always on the side of absolute truth. Much suspicion and at times paranoia was cast toward anyone outside the circle. Catholics, Muslims, and even the Methodists living next door all became suspect and an evangelism project.

I spent most of my growing up years in South Florida. The majority of my high school classmates were Catholic, Jewish, or "go to the beach on Sunday" people. Protestants were a minority. Within my Baptist church, I absorbed a message that there was "one way," and it was our particular way. Most of my closest friends wore a label different than my own. As I interacted with them, I felt confused. They were fun and smart and often true friends, but the ever present "in or out" mentality within erected barriers in our relationships. I could not relax, let down my guard, and enjoy those that my church labeled as "other."

At the same time, I witnessed several troubling situations and relationships within my church. Various shades of affairs and scandals came to light. One of my Sunday School teachers left his wife and family and created a new life with one of my teenage friends. I witnessed a youth minister tell one of my youth group friends that she had "bedroom eyes." Though I was uncomfortable at the time, it was years later that I realized he was saying that she had seductive eyes that expressed sexual longing. Were those of us inside the church really all that different? Did he take actions beyond using inappropriate words with my friend?

Despite internal uneasiness as I reached high school, college, and beyond, I nonetheless held onto the dogmas I had learned, and I operated adeptly within this system. I was afraid to step too far outside of this circle despite the internal misgivings I often experienced. Fear of "others" was ingrained in my mindset. There was much vocabulary around this idea, from fallen, to hell bound, to sinner. I preferred to view myself in the category of saint. Somehow acknowledging my very real struggles as a human being was a threat to the image I desired to transmit within my circle as well as out into the world. I preferred to wear masks and maintain my "safe" spot in the world of "the saved."

The emphasis on sporting a shiny and polished image over dealing with the oftentimes raw reality of the human experience led to an empty belief that how things look from the outside is of greater importance than what is truly going on inside. I embraced this mentality quite fully and successfully in many areas of life for many years. I knew how to make it all look fairly appealing and adeptly chose the correct mask to wear for any given situation. But there was a price to pay. An empty and hollow feeling often welled up as I struggled to figure out who indeed is the real Tricia. What do I actually believe or think about x, y, or z? Being mom to my hurting children was about to change all of this.

There were three solid years in a row where, every single night, one or both of our daughters woke up multiple times. Somewhere in the midst of this haze, I was sleeping on a mattress on the floor of their shared bedroom. One of the girls began crying and was inconsolable. I lost it. I screamed "shut up" as I shoved a pacifier into her mouth. Thankfully, I snapped back to reality within seconds, crumpled to the floor, and sobbed. I was exhausted, ashamed at my own behavior, and desperately in need of help. It felt like I was falling into a black hole with no way out. Though I didn't grasp it in the moment, this was an invitation to leave my circle, acknowledge my personal messiness, and accept my rightful place in fellowship with all of humanity.

Up until this night, something deep within me battled against speaking up and asking for help. My mind told me that

I should be able to handle things all by myself. Clearly, I reached a point where I could not. If I didn't change course, my children would continue to suffer. I didn't know how to help them.

This was the beginning of taking baby steps to get the assistance needed for such a complex season of parenting. My husband took turns with night duty, we reached out to professionals, and the seed was planted for the absolute necessity of self-care if there was any hope for our family to thrive. A way forward out of this dark place was elusive, but light and grace began shining through the cracks of my brokenness, making its way into my weary soul. The light began showing up in the darkness. In this broken state, I was in a posture that was ready to receive. Rather than identify myself as a set apart "righteous" person, I was now free to join in with all of humanity as someone in need of help.

As I wrote and re-wrote of this particular dark night, the daughter who was the object of my brokenness came to me and sat on my lap. "What are you writing about Mom?" I responded that there was something I wanted her to read. She read it. "What *exactly* did you say and do, Mom?" I told her every detail of the night when I emotionally snapped and shouted at her. She kind of giggled, though I assured her that it was no laughing matter. And then the power of secret shame and humiliation around this specific incident fell away. As I brought my own shame out of the darkness and into the light, it shattered into a thousand pieces.

If we are not willing to claim and acknowledge our transgressions, we perpetuate a cycle of anxiety, shame, and striving to have a glittering image even when we may be in reality falling apart. In the early days as mom to my daughters, my internal self contained an unsustainable mix. While I felt a great deal of guilt, fear, and shame, it was all tangled up with a righteous, "holier than thou" attitude. There were lessons I needed to learn about the multiple faces of shame.

Shame is a destructive and powerful five-letter word that resides deep within many a heart. "A fact or circumstance bringing disgrace or regret," says dictionary.com. Shame is often disguised under layer upon layer of pain and coping mechanisms, yet it is an invisible fire that burns and destroys. As it silently sets up camp in our souls, it then robs our joy and rightful place as beloved children of God. Its greatest ally is secrecy. Shame is most potently defeated by vulnerably sharing our stories of scandal and humiliation with fellow life journeyers whom we know to be trustworthy.

I know a thing or two about this silent thief. Our acquaintance began when as a child I assimilated the dominant message I heard in church. It was a message of right vs. wrong, good vs. bad, with a heavy dose of instruction on how to behave in a way to avoid the flames of hell. It seared my tender heart and contributed to making me a person full of fear and unacquainted with true grace. I lived in a state of dis-grace.

One day I spent several hours with my beautiful friend of fifteen plus years, Amy. Due to earthquake type circumstances in each of our lives, along with the natural shifts in life as children grow and circumstances change, we had not spent much recent time together. I unexpectedly showed up at her door with the intent to just drop off a birthday gift and quickly head home to a mountain of tasks awaiting me. The doorbell woke her from sleep, yet she graciously invited me into her cozy, well-loved home.

This friend has traveled a rough road. Chronic physical pain, a rip your heart out divorce, judgment from a pharisaical crowd, and life as a single mom are a few of the recent twists and turns in her life. She has a magnetic personality and is beautiful through and through, in both internal and external ways. In our heart to heart conversation, she said, "When I used to look at you, I saw you trying to be something that you were not. Now when I look at you, I see the real you, who you truly are." Her observations shed light on the person I used to project to the world, and words of grace were imparted as she acknowledged who I was becoming. While she may not know the specifics of my deepest struggles, she does have a heart that sees and knows others. We were real and vulnerable as we caught each other up on our lives, challenges, and joys.

As we were laying open our lives before one another, I sensed and then spoke that there seemed to be something deep down in her soul that did not believe she was a beloved and precious child of God. We were kindred spirits in that way. She took a deep breath, the tears began to flow, and then she told me her story. She was in college going on thirty years ago. She got pregnant. She had an abortion, all alone.

The palpable pain and suffering exposed in Amy's words and on her face wrecked me. The deepest source of pain seemed to be in the shame of having such a dark secret with no one to walk alongside and share the burden. This hidden wound had built up layers of shame, and the church that she was acquainted with was not a place to receive healing and grace on this matter. God forgive us.

As I look inward to the shame bearers in my life, they too have festered in the dark, hidden places of life. They flow from a place of doubt as to my rightful place as beloved by God. But my "go to" armor looks different than that of my precious friend who has felt less than and not good enough as a result of her secrets. Same shame, different response.

For years, my shame shield was much more about building up a wall of pride, arrogance, and self-righteousness while trying to make myself and others fit into a legalistic system or box. I was a Pharisee looking down on things from on high. The list of boxes I have tried out is long: correct theology, political affiliation, proper life choices, dietary habits, and economic systems. If I could set up a system where I am "in" and "right," then anything outside of my box could be viewed as "out" and "wrong." This led to a glittering but false image that I projected to the world. My heart was full of judgment toward others. I lived in a shame filled place of great frustration as my inside longings and outside life did not match.

As I embrace my rightful place as a complicated and messy human being, healing as well as a joyful pursuit of true abundant life are realized. The truth is that I, just like my friend Amy, never actually felt good enough, but I camouflaged it with pride and arrogance. My new desire is to be a person who can receive with grace and mercy the dark secrets of others and walk alongside without judgment or trying to save or fix. I want to be a traveler through life who can share my own shame and secrets with trustworthy fellow sojourners, embracing together Jesus' words, "You will know the truth and the truth will set you free."

Recently, my husband, daughters, and I were skyping with one of our sons. This big brother imparted great wisdom to his little sisters. "When I was your age, I thought that our family had it all together. Other people really looked up to us. Now I know that we are just as messed up as everyone else." Truth.

I'm learning to be honest with myself, with God, and then with others as I pursue intimate acquaintance with the messiness and shame that resides within. It takes courage. It hurts. But when I am honest and real about those things that humiliate me, the power of shame is destroyed. I am then free to be genuine and sincere about the good and bad intermingled within me. I am set free to live as one with an open heart. I am able to be more real about the complexities of my choices and actions, even the decision to adopt our daughters.

At this point in my journey, I feel embarrassed when I think back to my earliest perspective and reasons for becoming an adoptive mom. As the voices within American evangelicalism called loudly for Christians to adopt, many responded. Organized movements such as Orphan Sundays continue to take place in many evangelical churches every year. A brand of Christian colonialism is often a part of the message. The call to adopt is sometimes hailed as a way to "save the children" in both pragmatic and spiritual ways. There are beautiful stories of welcoming children into family, culture, and religion. However, many of these stories have a self congratulatory spin and paint an incomplete picture. They rarely give honor to the devastation and pain that are the foundation of the experience for any adopted child or birth parent.

The underlying realities, forces, and stories that make up each individual adoption scenario are extremely complex. The reasons that a child ends up unable to grow up with their birth family or in their birth country are many. None of the explanations are happy. Often the evangelical call to adoption glosses over this truth. As I approached the idea of adoption, I did not fully comprehend the underlying devastation of the story I was about to join.

When we set out to adopt a child, I did my homework on various international adoption programs as well as the US foster care system. I was well aware that certain countries had ethically questionable practices. But China seemed different. The one-child policy coupled with a cultural preference for sons enabled a more tidy narrative about the girls available for adoption in a country halfway around the world. In hindsight, that was not the full reality. I actually participated in something much more complicated.

Whenever western money and power enter into a place with economic struggles, complications and corruption are sure to follow. A most crass form of supply and demand, or more accurately demand then supply, did on some level become a part of the overarching adoption story in China. In some cases, the realities of child trafficking and kidnapping became a dark underside of a seemingly "clean" international adoption program.[7]

It is deeply painful to admit that I was in any way a participant in such a heartbreaking story. Even if my individual children have a different specific story, on some level I still contributed to the circumstances that have become a part of a larger narrative of adoption that includes corruption and trafficking. I have had to reckon with the reality that all of my intentions aside, I personally and corporately participated in a great darkness.

Some would argue that there is nothing to be gained from bringing up such a delicate and pain filled topic. I disagree. This is a very real aspect of our daughters' possible stories. Chances are that we will never know the full details behind each of their individual early lives, but they too are part of a larger narrative. If they can use Google, which they most certainly can, they will know. I believe that it is my responsibility to introduce to them, in age appropriate ways, this heart-wrenching shadow of an oft prettified face of adoption, before they are blindsided by it from some other source.

I remember when one of our girls was in kindergarten, she came home one day and said this: "Molly in my class said that the mommies and daddies in China love their boys more than their girls. Is that true?" I honestly thought that I had more time before she would be confronted with some of the cultural realities that may or may not have led to her landing in an American family across the world from where she was born. I wanted to be the one to introduce her to the nuances and complexities around this idea. But on that day, I did the best I could to begin the lifelong conversation around why and how and for what reason she ended up in our family. The conservative Christian go-to narrative when life gets complicated is often, "it's all part of God's plan." That wasn't going to cut it here. And what adopted child would then decide to trust a God like that?

When I first began to awaken to the underside of the China adoption program, I felt physically ill and had to wrestle with and slowly let the realities seep into my mind, heart, and soul. The truth is that I don't have satisfactory answers nor can I spin out a story to my daughters that denies the very real human suffering that is an integral part of each and every adoption story. It is a tale that includes individual blindness, collective greed, and the entanglement of two very different cultures.

One place that I often turn to for perspective is the voices of adult adoptees. Liz Latty shares these powerful words: ". . . I began to dream in earnest about what it would be like for adoptees to exist in a world that understands the paradoxical experiences that we live. A world that does not insist on reducing us to cheerful assumptions and sentimental media representations. A world that accepts adoption not as an unquestionable, benevolent good, not as a fairy tale ending, but as an event that forever changes and complicates the lives of everyone involved. That when the gavel crashes into the sounding block, literally or symbolically, it is both a fracturing and a coming together, a severing and a multiplication, a derailment and a hope for the uncertain path ahead."[8]

Latty's words point toward the truth that grace and redemption are most often woven throughout adoption. But the cost of true redemption is scorned when the foundational pain and loss of each and every adoptee and birth parent are ignored. Adoption narratives that tell only the joyful side of the story somehow cheapen the grace intermingled in such journeys. Painful beginnings are the foundation that must be given honor as we seek to make meaning of such stories. As mom, I need to own my role as well as be as honest as possible about the nuances, complications, and missing pieces that make up the mystery of the early lives of my daughters. It is not a simple story that can be brushed over with tales of airport welcome home parties, adoption day celebrations, and God's will. The reality is much more complex.

On the anniversary of our daughters' adoptions, we remember and celebrate as a family. One piece of this tradition is to watch a video created from footage shot on each of their adoption trips. As each adoption day comes, it gets harder and harder for me to watch the videos. As I experienced each of these journeys, my joy and personal perspective clouded the reality of what was happening to each of my girls. Now, as I am confronted with these images, I see the grief, sadness, and sorrow in their little faces. Their world was being turned upside down once again on the day that we adopted them.

During a recent Christmas holiday, our family sat down to share our girls' adoption videos with their new sister-in-law. One of our sons silently sobbed as he watched. He later told me that the realities of birth parents, power inequities, privilege, and all of the messy human realities involved in this exchange overwhelmed him. This big brother absolutely adores his sisters, and I speculate that he cannot imagine our collective family life without them. They have graced us with much joy, fun, growth, and laughter. As I looked into his face, I saw a kindred spirit who is wrestling with the reality that a full and mindful life as a human being is both complicated and messy.

Do I believe that all children deserve to live and grow up within a family? Yes. But I also must be mindful and realistic about the pain, suffering, and sometimes dark side of extremely complicated situations. Adoption is not always the answer nor is it an action that covers over all the pain that has come before it.

Within the conservative Christian world, I sometimes hear "God loves adoption." Though I am a solid believer that any life or journey or action can be redeemed, I do not believe that God simply loves adoption. I imagine that the relay of loss that is triggered at the beginning of any adoption story breaks the heart of the divine. I do believe that adoption is sometimes the best way forward in the midst of devastating circumstances. There are three perspectives in each and every adoption scenario - the child, the birth parent, and the adoptive parent. All must be considered and given honor as life altering decisions are made. There are no absolutes. I do believe in beauty from ashes and the ever-present possibility of redemption and hope.

As opposed to the overly tidy narrative of "God loves adoption," perhaps there is a more complex perspective. At the core of the Christian faith is the story of God's redeeming acts toward humans. I do not believe that God rejoices when a parent is unable to raise their child, no matter the reason. I imagine that God is broken hearted when a child loses her parents and then suffers and struggles to adjust to a new home. But despite the turmoil that we as humans create, God is at work. It seems more authentic to say "God loves redemption." My desire is that as my daughters examine their life stories, they will know a measure of redemption. There is no question that their entrance into our family was the gateway to true redemption for me.

Which of us enjoys looking at our own personal dark sides and being candid about what we find? I don't. Yet with experience and practice, I have learned that being real about and facing my shadow life puts it into perspective. Sharing shame and regret out loud to myself, my God, and then sometimes to others is cleansing. Confession is indeed good for the soul. We aren't alone. We all have secrets, thoughts, or actions that would be mortifying to lay bare before others.

One day while sharing breakfast with one of our sons, he expressed his distaste for hanging out with those who seem to be "squeaky clean." "I like people with dirt around the edges," he said. The truth is that all of our edges are dirty, but some of us just work harder to appear clean and sparkly as we present a pretty package for others to behold. Yet the reality is that wearing masks is exhausting. I know this first hand. It has been quite freeing to claim my rightful place among those with dirt around the edges.

When we think we are somehow special and immune from participation in our world's darkness, we isolate ourselves, set up a false façade, and live exhausting and unsustainable lives. But if we wallow in the dark, it leads to despair. There is a middle way. For me, it began with the acceptance that I am fully human and no different from any other being walking this planet. Such a perspective and the acknowledgement of my own shadow side readied my soul to start receiving true grace. It started with giving this gift to myself.

Reflection

After exhausting decades of trying to appear as though I have my act together, I can now rest. I am fully human and have a shadow side. I am fully loved and have the capacity to shine light out into the world. I have finally found the place of "like running through a field."

CHAPTER 4

⊙⊙⊙⊙

SURRENDER TO SELF-CARE

Are you tired? Worn out? Burned out on religion? Come to me. Get away with me and you'll recover your life. I'll show you how to take a real rest. Walk with me and work with me. Watch how I do it. Learn the unforced rhythms of grace. I won't lay anything heavy or ill-fitting on you. Keep company with me and you'll learn to live freely and lightly.
Matthew 11:28-30, The Message

In the early days of family with three sons, we fell into routines. For about ten years as I turned thirty and then forty, life with our three sons rolled along. Mark worked long hours and traveled frequently. I took pride in my independence and ability to "keep it all afloat" on the home front. Sometimes friends and I would look askance at moms who needed more hands on help from their husbands. My own blurred sense of self and family allowed me to see myself as having it all together. We had a traditional division of labor, and I settled into the role of stay-at-home mom.

My natural inclination was to live life in the fast lane. That looked something like this: volunteer everywhere my kids are involved and places beyond; take on leadership roles at school and church; have kids signed up for multiple activities at a time requiring carpools, driving back and forth across town, and lots of coordination; fit in a few exercise sessions a week; do a Bible study; squeeze in errands; throw something to eat on the table; and fall into bed exhausted every night. I remember at lunchtime the five to ten minutes required to make a healthy salad was too demanding, and I rarely sat down to eat. I was an oxymoron. A stay-at-home mom on a grab and go meal plan as I bounced from activity to responsibility to meeting.

When raising our sons, I lived this pace of life. There were exceptions, but overall I believed I was juggling a lot without dropping too many balls. Unacknowledged anxiety was my ever-present companion, and I used busyness to drown out its voice and warning signals. Mind-body connection was a foreign concept. My physical body was in fact sending out warning signs, but I was deaf to them. Looking back, I shake my head, in an endearing sort of way, and stand amazed at the level of unconsciousness around my choices. My supermom complex was alive and well. Such a pace is sustainable for only a short time. It was about to catch up with me.

As I took on the demands of five children, multiplied by the special needs of our two daughters, my body began to break down. In the winter of 2007, freshly recovered from mononucleosis due to exhaustion, my back started to scream out to me with excruciating pain. At that point in life, I had an uncanny ability to ignore the early warning signs that my body spoke. A forty-four year old mom to children aged 3, 4, 14, 17 and 19 years old, I was falling apart both physically and emotionally. The back pain practically immobilized me. I have a vivid memory of hobbling up to preschool with my daughters. I could barely make it. An acquaintance looked at me and said, "What is wrong with you? You look awful." After preschool drop off, I would head straight home and lie on a wicker sofa on our back porch. It was the one place that I could get relief from the pain. I tried a myriad of interventions to no avail, and surgery was scheduled for early June.

My ruptured disc was repaired but then re-ruptured a mere day or two after surgery. One night in the midst of one-week apart back surgeries, God and I had a wrestling match, all night long. I felt like Jacob and the angel from the Old Testament. A friend gave me the book *Left to Tell: Discovering God Amidst the Rwandan Holocaust* by Immaculeé Ilibagiza. This book along with chapters 40 and up from the prophet Isaiah became a wrestling mat. Surrender was the message that kept pinning me down. I am a fighter, and I don't go down easily.

As I literally rolled around the bed writhing in both physical and emotional pain, the word surrender came into my heart and mind over and over again. Clearly my lifestyle choices were not working. I was drowning and feared that the rest of the family was going down with me. I did not fully understand what it was that I needed to yield to, but I was convinced that I needed to wave a white flag and head in a different direction. I had literally come to a place in life where my lifestyle choices had broken my back. Twice.

As I began the long, slow road of physical rehabilitation and walked for short periods, multiple times a day, surrender became my heartbeat and prayer. I would say the word over and over again. A gentle beckoning within and without shed light on a better way to live. A posture of giving up my old ways was the first step in a slow turning toward wholeness and health.

My husband adapted his work schedule to be more hands-on at home. My parents, who are really great at showing up, came in and out of our home during this time to help care for me and our children. Friends stepped up and provided food and encouragement. My mother-in-law flew down and helped out. We hired someone to do the day-to-day care of our children while I focused on rest and recovery.

Because I needed to put my energy toward getting well, a rotation of family and hired sitters was put in place to care for our daughters. One day I left to go on a short rehab walk and returned to our home. Our four year-old girl was standing in the driveway sobbing. "Mommy, I thought you weren't coming back." My heart broke. Another day, the girls and their babysitter made a huge "get well soon" chalk drawing on our driveway. I longed to be the one hanging out with my daughters. I had a lot of time to consider how to make amends and change course.

I was in need of an extreme makeover. Anne Lamott says, "When you become desperate, you become teachable."[9] I was in the primary days of self-care school.

To be clear, the term self-care is not an endorsement of a lifestyle that mirrors the Vogue or Cosmopolitan covers that I walk by and read over in check out lines and doctor's offices. American lifestyle values so often emphasize various flavors of extreme. On one hand, there is pressure for perfection in the area of our physical bodies that leads to intense emphasis on fitness, clothing, leisure, and other material pursuits. We also value an uber Puritan work ethic that espouses the idea that the one who is busiest and sacrifices most is superior. The command to remember the Sabbath is so often ignored.

It used to be that something deep in my gut hitched and rebelled whenever I heard others encourage me toward, or even just suggest the general idea of the importance of taking care of self. Something in my brain screamed "you're selfish," "you don't deserve that," or some other degrading message. Role models and faith models did not encourage a self-care point of view, and in fact they often demonstrated a "give until you drop dead" lifestyle.

My earliest arguments against the idea of self-care were born from a conflict between faith values and the worship-of-self values in culture. The Puritan work ethic was embedded in my mindset. The "Give your all and sacrifice until it hurts" messages resounded within. Most forms of self-care felt selfish and somehow wrong to me.

I love massages and find them very relaxing. They soothe both my body and anxiety prone mind. But whenever I thought about caring for myself in this way, the anti self-care messages in my head cranked up to high volume. When I did allow myself to actually get on the massage table, I would take pains to hide it from others. In the early days of my self-care conversion, I told one mental health therapist that I had begun to schedule monthly massages. She was privy to the details of our challenging family life and suggested that it might make more sense for me to have weekly massage appointments. That felt much too indulgent. Simmering and sometimes overwhelming guilt arose whenever I participated in something that even resembled caring for myself. A change of heart and mind had now become a necessity.

The reality is that anyone involved in caretaking must prioritize care of self if they desire to live as a healthy human being. Each and every parent falls into the definition of caretaker. And during times of intensive and stressful care of others, the need for such cushion and space becomes even more critical. Despite my adept denial ability, I was clearly involved in intense and complex parenting during these days.

Yet I still clung to my old "I can handle it all" mindset. The falling apart of my body, emotions, and spirit was a deep and wide invitation to wake up and take steps to prioritize care for myself.

I was missing a critical truth of being human. Parker J. Palmer says it like this. "Self-care is never a selfish act-it is simply good stewardship of the only gift I have, the gift I was put on earth to offer others. Anytime we can listen to true self and give the care it requires, we do it not only for ourselves, but for the many others whose lives we touch."[10]

In my attempts to be super human, I worked and busied myself into a state of both physical and emotional inaccessibility. As I spent days laid up on a couch exhausted by mono, writhing in pain, or recovering from double back surgery, I had little to offer to my family or friends. Rather I created a scenario that imposed a huge emotional and physical drain upon my family. Sometimes things happen that are out of our control, and everyone must adapt and dig deeper. This was not one of those times. My personal choices and lack of self-awareness lured me down a path toward ruin. I am grateful that this painful wake-up call demanded my attention. Thus began a journey that continues to this day.

As I recovered from back surgery, I began to take baby steps toward healthy self-care. It was a multi-pronged approach. Exercise, diet, mental health, and the exploration of my own life giving pursuits all called for my attention. Exercise became a priority as I more fully listened to the memo that my broken back had delivered. Running was no longer a good option, but walking and yoga called my name. I was convinced that taking the time to shop, chop, and eat healthy foods was necessary, and I committed to sitting down during the lunch hour. I began to accept the reality that anxiety was affecting my sleep. I was honest with my doctor and took medication for a season as a stop gap in a time of crisis. It bought me time until I could more holistically deal with this unwanted companion. Even today, I have an anxiety "rescue medication" that I take as needed. I gave myself permission to seek and explore various leisure pursuits as I figured out what filled my soul. I began to practice the discipline of paying attention to the whispers of both body and soul as I move through life. It was the beginning of a slow awakening.

I have noticed that within many of the Christian contexts of my life, there is great reluctance, and even stigma, associated with giving voice to authentic struggles and seeking professional help. This seems particularly true when the topic of mental health or difficulties with a child are involved. Do we sometimes think God should be sufficient for absolutely everything, and we are failures if we need this kind of help? Are we afraid of what others will think or say about us if they find out? Is it that we are admitting some kind of defeat or weakness of character when we reach out for help? I am sure there are myriad thoughts and reasons around this. Maybe the American values of being self-made and self-sufficient are all tangled up in it.

I think back to two conversations that I had during the early years of my self-care awakening. The first was with a minister friend who expressed something along the lines of "Surely there are other people in this church who have struggles with their children—why don't we talk to each other about this?" In another conversation, a minister's spouse told me that she and her husband had been going to see a therapist. She recounted that she had been quite honest and open as she interacted with others, since her perspective was that this was a healthy and helpful thing to do for her marriage and family. She was puzzled and surprised by people who literally came and whispered in her ear or called her later. In hushed voices, they asked her questions as though it was something that could not be spoken of out loud. Her friends needed help too, but they were afraid, ashamed, or somehow needed permission from the minister's family to go and get that help.

A third conversation happens regularly with a number of mom friends. After taking the initial step into the doors of a mental health professional, each of these friends has recounted something like this: "There were a lot of families in the waiting room, and some were people that I know. There are a lot of us." We are not alone.

By the time our daughters were in preschool, I had definitely surrendered to the idea that mental health professionals could be extremely helpful. I had already experienced this when our son struggled with anxiety in the third grade. There were challenges with our daughters that required this type of support. I realized that rather than interpreting the need for mental health services as a weakness, it was in fact a relief and a healthy support. But it was only after my own unraveling that I was ready to participate in such help for myself. As I came face to face with my own limitations as a mom, rather than just sending my children to therapy when things got out of control, I joined in. Our family is a system, and I play a critical role. Looking back over the last ten years, it is possibly the single most important gift of self-care that I have given to myself.

In Ecclesiastes, it says, "Though one may be overpowered, two can defend themselves. A cord of three strands is not quickly broken" (Ecclesiastes 4:12). I've always envisioned God in that mix of three, but I also know that another person is a part of that cord as well. Out of love for myself and my family, when it was time, I sought professional help. I have experienced deep joy and pain as I explore both struggles and triumphs with a trusted counselor. It was such a relief to realize that neither I nor my children need to navigate the bumps in life alone.

Colliding head on with my physical and emotional limitations as a human and a mother was a life-giving invitation to participate in true care of myself. In an almost ten year slow and steady change of direction, I am well on my way to discovering that which satisfies. If you had asked me ten years ago what created passion within Tricia Wilson, I would have come up empty. I had no idea.

One of my favorite hymn refrains proclaims the beautiful words, "it is well with my soul." Though often played at funerals, it seems that this posture is just as critical for the living as the dead. For me, it has taken time and intention to discover that which fills my soul.

As a younger person, most of my time and energy was consumed with being mom, keeping a household running, and being volunteer extraordinaire. In hindsight, it is easy to identify personal needs that were met in this action packed role, but they had nothing to do with soul filling. Achievement desires, anxiety management, feelings of obligation, people pleasing, and a desire to be important and make a difference were among the reasons that I poured so much of myself into these commitments.

And though some of the above goals were realized, my soul was not satisfied. For the most part, I do not regret the time and energy spent there, because it was an important leg of a journey. Learning what is life sucking rather than life giving is critical to begin the shift toward true peace and joy.

I recently received a gift: the realization that after much hard work, I am well on my way to discovering the specific things that fill my soul. It was at the end of a week away with part of our family. Time together was soul filling, to a point. After a little too much together time and the realization that the next two days would include times with four people in a small, intimate hotel room, I realized that I needed to figure out a way to recharge. As the rest of the family headed to a football game, I asked myself, "what can I do to fill my soul?" for the next six hours.

It was a beautiful New England day, so I decided to jump onto the T and head somewhere that I had never been before: Cambridge, the home of Harvard University. First stop was a yoga studio where my body and spirit were renewed. Then an unhurried walk around a beautiful university campus, followed by the discovery of a fun and delicious local eating place with a book in hand. Though the original thought was to take public transportation back to downtown Boston, the weather and something internal beckoned me to instead start walking the four miles back. I passed beautiful historical homes, an ethnic neighborhood, a financial district, and crossed a bridge while gazing out at a stunning cityscape. It was six hours well spent.

It has taken time and experimentation to discover the things that are truly life giving for me. A critical step in this discovery was to clear away the things that had become burdensome and joy stealing. All of the volunteering and busyness blurred my vision and prevented me from seeing what matters most. A few things that quench my personal heart thirst are writing, listening to authors tell their stories, one on one time with my husband, listening to interesting podcasts, receiving communion, reading, doing yoga, indie movies, meditation, walking, and treading water with a friend. It is a gift to enjoy my own company as well as that of others.

Times of transition provide opportunities to explore and discover what it is that makes us soar. I imagine that when there is more time and space and less active parenting, a certain type of volunteering will be a part of my soul care. Those who face a few extra hours when they experience a job or career shift, as children head to school, or as they approach an empty nest are afforded new opportunities to discover what it is that gives life and contentment. It will look different for each of us.

Early one morning, I trekked to one of my least favorite bi-yearly events: a dental check up. I had the same dental hygienist for the first twenty-four years that I lived in this city. She worked in this one office for over forty-seven years and has known no other lifestyle in her adult life. This was our last scheduled interaction as she was set to retire at the end of the year. She became teary as we communicated around this topic, and my words to her were, "I hope that you discover what you love to do outside of these walls." After these words left my mouth, I realized something very important. With a great deal of intention and hard work, the former walls that contained me had fallen apart. I had truly discovered that which fills my soul.

As I made way for self-care and created space to discover my passions, I also became better able to tolerate my accountability in problematic family interactions. I have slowly but surely taken responsibility for my role in our particular family dynamics. There aren't many parenting paradigms that emphasize behavioral changes required of the grown ups in a family. Most of them are focused on changing the behavior of the child. Self-care gave me the capacity to grow and change. It strengthened me as I moved toward more fully taking ownership in the parent-child dance.

Reflection

Dear Tricia,

You are beloved. You are known fully. Just like each and every human person, you are a complex mix. Good and bad all entangled together. You do not have to strive. You can rest. You are enough. You are loved.

Your true self (and I'm pretty sure God would sign off on this as well)

CHAPTER 5

⬤⬤⬤⬤⬤

OWNING MY PART

Attack the evil that is within yourself,
rather than attacking the evil that is in others.
Confucius

One Mother's Day, I received a public Facebook message from our eldest child. He referred to me as "trill." After I consulted my handy Google urban dictionary to determine if this was an insult or compliment, I realized that it was high praise. "True + real = trill. Meaning someone that always keeps it 100 at all times, stays true to oneself, and stays real no matter what happens to the end." Wow, what a compliment and a standard that in daily living I struggle to embody.

It is a gift of grace when someone who has hurt us owns the truth and is trill about that. Genuine apologies are restorative. My college fellowship leader who insisted that immature students sign agreement to the "Chicago Statement on Biblical Inerrancy," comes to mind. After I left this university and over many years, I heard murmurings and friends of friends of friends reporting that he experienced great pain and suffering within his family. One year, around homecoming weekend, there was a widespread invitation to a reunion of this Christian group. Several friends reported back a poignant moment of humility and grace. This same man, about twenty years later and softened by grief, came before many of the young and impressionable hearts he had coerced. He apologized. He was trill. He made amends. Resentment that I felt toward him softened and melted away.

The journey to becoming trill with myself around the subject of parenting is ongoing. I desire to live into that Mother's Day compliment, and I am making slow yet steady progress. After my physical breakdown, and as I began to pick up the pieces within our family and find a way forward, I needed to be honest and real. It was time to put a magnifying glass up to my role in the struggles happening in my family. The areas requiring honest inspection were many. My list included: the parenting roles my husband and I chose, mothering choices, my emotional challenges, and how a number of my personal decisions affected my children. In order to move ahead, I had to own my part.

Much of the parenting advice floating around, and certainly the ideas most proclaimed within evangelical Christendom, address the how-to and specific formulas for making a child's behavior change and adapt to the parent's wishes. I have come across very little that puts the burden of change upon the parent in order to have healthy family interactions. Because my old go-to parenting formulas were breaking down, I had to find a new way to interact with my children. Introspection and genuine soul searching were in order.

When life experiences beg me to "look in the mirror," I often balk. It was much more comfortable back in the day when I could look at my child and his behavior as completely his responsibility. I find it challenging to look at my own baggage, issues, and what I bring to the table as a parent.

Religious dogmatism trained me to place high value on being right. By default, anyone with a different opinion, perspective, or belief was wrong. Our way is best, and we have it all worked out and justified. It is so much easier to look at all of life from my own perspective. Self-questioning and reflection are tough. Sure, I will make the occasional apology to my child when my behavior crosses into hurtful and out of line territory. But to truly examine myself, as well as seek out the particular role I play in any difficult interactions with those I live with, takes guts. It is a painfully slow process. In fact, once I chose to venture down this path, it became a lifelong journey.

When one of our children displays extreme behaviors or a challenging temperament, I've been tempted to make that child a scapegoat. The origin of the word scapegoat comes from the Hebrew word *azazel*. Around the Jewish Day of

Atonement, this goat was sent out into the wilderness bearing the sins of God's people. A dictionary definition for scapegoat is "a person [or goat] made to bear the blame for others."[11]

My mind wanders back to the time period when our then third grade son experienced anxiety that interfered with his and our family's everyday life. I rejected the gentle prodding of his counselor to look at my role in this troubling dynamic. I preferred to make my son a scapegoat. This was his problem. I wasn't ready to own my part.

The reality is that in a family, we are all intimately tangled up together. The way that I as a parent respond to and approach the world affects my children, their felt safety, and the way that they respond and behave in the world. If I adhere to an a+b=c formulaic parenting method and one of our kids isn't jiving with this formula, the temptation is to cast blame onto them. How can I ask a child to own responsibility for her own behavior if I am not willing to do so myself? I am the adult. The burden is on me.

Over the years as different members of our family moved in and out of the offices of various mental health professionals, I heard a recurring term - the "identified client." This is a code word for "the kid whose behavior is wreaking havoc within the family and got this family into my office." One child therapist told me that with most families, once she begins to gently push on the idea that the parents are also in need of professional counsel and change, they disappear. As I began to comprehend the subtle message that the therapists were communicating, I felt defensive. "Is she saying that I am making my kid a scapegoat?" "Do *I* need to be the client?"

Over time, I let this profound message sink into my heart. My child may be the client who is identified, but I as the parent in the mix need to take a long hard look at myself and figure out how I need to adapt in order to lead our family down a healing path. I may not currently be the one "identified" but I am nonetheless a critical component of a system in need of change. In fact, *I* needed to get myself into a therapeutic relationship and take my rightful place as the "identified client." As I admitted my own need for help and embraced the hard work of change, the benefits spilled out onto the whole family. When I am healthier, those I am in relationship are also healthier.

At one point in our family's journey and after several of our children had been in and out of therapy at different points along the way, my husband looked at me and said, "Looks like we are the only two left in therapy." I wonder how the story might have twisted and what pain might have been avoided if we had been the first to go there rather than the last.

When relationships become difficult, a first step forward is to look honestly at our role in any troubling family or life dynamic. Most of us benefit from exploring such matters in the company of a counselor or therapist. Despite the message that I took in from many Christians that needing help of this sort demonstrates some type of character flaw or lack of faith, my experience has been quite the opposite. It is both a gift and a privilege to be in such a therapeutic relationship. It takes great strength, honesty, and a letting go of less than functional coping mechanisms to approach my specific role in any challenging situation or relationship. Professionals have supported me as I come to terms with many uncomfortable and painful truths about myself and those I love. I have often felt a great deal more grace "on the couch" than "in the pew."

When I first began to walk this path of self-examination and owning my role in the family dynamic, I was often tempted to sink into a place of guilt, defeat, and a feeling of helplessness. The good news is that God puts us together in families for incredibly redemptive purposes. It is never too late to work on relationship. As I began to loosen up, look closer at myself, and work to change where needed, it led to healing conversations with my children, even my grown children. Each family member, whether "identified" or not, has more space to "own our part." There is no longer a need or desire for a family scapegoat. We each have equal voice and value. When I let go of pointing fingers and casting blame, I was then free to begin the long journey toward changing myself and the ways that I interacted with my family.

Because I was the primary hands-on parent for many years, there was a great deal in this particular area that I needed to examine and own. As I began a slow awakening to the necessity for a parenting paradigm shift, I had little idea of what to do. In 2008 my friend Holly invited me to be a part of a support group of amazing adoptive moms. Still in a great deal of denial about the broken state of my own self and family, I pushed her off and rationalized that, "Her family may be really struggling, but ours is doing well enough. We don't need *that* kind of help. We aren't as messed up or dysfunctional as they are..." My expertise was in seeing the messiness in others while putting up blinders to it within my own self and family. My work of becoming fully human was still in an early stage. But the reality was that at home there were behavioral challenges and escalating situations that were totally out of my parental control. I needed help.

During this time I was still battling the inner voices in support of the formulaic conservative Christian parenting methods I had practiced with our sons. I needed courage to go against methods that had been presented as "God's true way." I had no clue as to a healthy way forward. My false facade of self-sufficiency in the role of mom added to my reluctance to join up with other struggling moms. Pride and arrogance with a heavy dose of denial kept me isolated as I bought a lie that I could and should do this all by myself. As I continued to attempt to pick up the pieces after my back surgeries, a first step was to acknowledge that my former ways had obviously led to a level of destruction both in my physical body and my family. My heart and mind continued to crack open.

After finally admitting that my mom skills needed an overhaul, I decided to give this group of moms a try. It couldn't hurt… As both a support group and a place to learn new ways of parenting together, this gathering became foundational for a great deal of future change within me. Each group member had bought into the conservative Christian parenting paradigm on some level and was living day by day the painful limits of such an approach. As adoptive moms, we were all in over our heads and desperate for a way forward. Several of us experienced judgment from our communities of faith. Our kids were not fitting into the formula.

We joined hearts and hands as we studied and discussed new approaches to being parents and interacting with our hurting children. For two school years in a row, several of us met weekly to study, apply, and encourage one another to change both heart and mind around matters of parenting. We studied Becky Bailey's *Conscious Discipline* workbook weekly for one year and then did it all again the following year. A great deal of hard work and intention is required to change a mind as well as a parenting pattern. We walked alongside each other through medication decisions, therapy, hospitalizations, residential treatment programs, and the everyday ups and downs of parenting children affected by trauma.

With the support of this group, I made great strides toward changing my beliefs, skills, and behavior in the midst of a season of complex parenting. We spoke of our deepest fears and received each other's pain. We served as cheerleaders to one another as each of us traveled our own specific paths with our own specific children. We often role played out loud new ways of interacting with our kids. As I pursued a radical renewal of mind and heart, I found the capacity to make lasting change. This happened as I acknowledged my very real need for others to walk alongside me on this journey. I no longer viewed such support as a weakness but as a gift. There was no reason for me to be alone in this pursuit.

For a season of about four years, we met together regularly. But as always, life transitions and our needs change. We only meet once in a great while these days, but each time we cross paths, we experience a safe and grace filled bond with one another. I have much gratitude for these women who encouraged me to become a better mom. We learned many new skills together. I carried these new ideas into our home, and my husband began to see positive results within our changing family dynamic. Gratefully, I was not walking this journey alone. I had a partner.

When our family began to fall apart in obvious ways, there was an invitation for my husband Mark and me to engage in conversation around our marriage roles and how we could each adapt to meet the needs of our family. My "I can handle it all" belief around being mom and home manager played a large part in a stark division of labor within our home. I pretty much handled all matters at home, and Mark took care of work and financial provision. Though his work was demanding, he did spend a good deal of his free time interacting with our children. He always had more energy and patience with play activity, and he pulled his weight when there were mini crises along the parenting way. But the day-to-day myriad of details and tasks involving children and home mostly fell to me. Sometimes when he pitched in on the mundane day-to-day tasks, I was critical and frustrated that he didn't do it "my way." I needed to release control and accept that there is more than one way to load a dishwasher...

On reflection, I wish that a more integrated partnership had been a conscious and discussed desire during the early days of a now thirty-three year marriage. The reality is that it took us over thirty years to navigate and negotiate a more intentional side-by-side relationship. I wasn't even particularly aware of my own desires in this area. The reasons for this are many, yet I am grateful for the ongoing journey to a place of more satisfying partnership.

In April of 2015, we celebrated a milestone event for Mark and his career. He stepped aside from the role of chairman of his company and began a several years long ramping down of the time that he spends at work. Though he is not yet retiring, his focus is in transition. This was a much planned for adjustment from both the home and work sides of the equation. Our family is already enjoying the many benefits of this decision.

When we dated and dreamed of our married days, it was always my wish to stay at home with children. I have kind of made a career of it! Some mothers have this same desire and choose to do so. Others love to work and choose that path. Necessity and the stream of bills sometimes leave parents with little choice but to have two parents at work. Personally, I have great respect and admiration for each path taken and the highest regard for parents going it alone without a partner.

In our home, because of the demands of the work that Mark chose, my choice to be at home has worked best. Along the way I have exercised my own gifts and talents in various volunteer spaces and places. I am extremely grateful for the resources, experiences, and people that we have met in connection with his company.

Yet, my personal relationship with this job is a bit complicated. Sometimes I have felt jealous and resentful of the time, energy, and travel required of him. At the same time, there is great joy in seeing him flourish in a place where he is able to utilize his talents and gifts. I have felt tired and lonely when he is out of town but have also delighted in the fact that he has had a career that is fulfilling and challenging year after year. The mere fact that his pay more than allows me the choice of holding down the Wilson fort is a gift. I have mixed emotions for sure.

I recently heard my mom once again say something like, "When I was in college, most women had the choice between being a teacher or a nurse." Both are wonderful professions, but not for everyone. My mom would have made a wonderful architect... When I was in college, there were certainly broader options for women, but the challenges to fulfill career and family dreams simultaneously remained. This tension is still with us. Most of us can't "have it all."

During the recent April milestone weekend, Mark and I were blindsided by a beautiful and touching recognition of his leadership role and my support of him in that pursuit. It was humbling and emotional. Much is a blur, but my proudest moment was when he was referred to as a servant leader, one thing about him that I deeply love and respect. There is something incredibly attractive about seeing a grown man choke up and cry. Most of us don't get standing ovations from a big room full of people. It was an honor to share the spotlight with him on that night.

Getting to the decision for my husband to begin to step away from a demanding profession and move toward home has been quite a process. It has required a great deal of honest communication. Sometimes words are spoken in love, sometimes in desperation, and hopefully always with respect along with open ears and hearts. At times it has felt like a great big negotiation full of compromise from each side.

Work-life balance is challenging. One of my favorite moments during the weekend was an exchange I had with two company employee dads. "We make it a priority to show up at our children's schools each and every week for an hour. Yes, we miss work, but we figure out a way to make that up." This was not the mentality of the mostly male leaders of my husband's company in days gone by. It is also exciting to see more females in a company that has traditionally been predominantly male. I have seen flexibility and progress in this area during the twenty-five plus years since Mark began his work in that place.

As I reflect on the emotions and the observations from that April weekend, hope arises. I have a great deal of optimism for both our daughters and our sons as they move toward work-life balance and choices. I hope that their choices will be broader and approached with greater imagination and the careful consideration of both partners' wishes and dreams, whatever they may be. I feel optimism that each will have voice and choice in the path forward for their individual families.

My husband's company is quite mindful that the time and energy required of its employees has an impact on the children and spouses in each family story. They often express gratitude for sacrifices made. On the 2015 Saturday night when I was asked to share the spotlight, I received beautiful flowers with this note attached, "Behind every good man is a great woman. Thank you." From their perspective, I am certainly behind the scenes. There isn't much immediate gratification nor glory in my chosen profession. And I truly appreciate the acknowledgement that his career path has been a team effort.

But in this next season of life, I hope that at its close, Mark and I can write this to each other: "Alongside every good partner is another." That is our desire for this next phase as we move toward the owning of our choices as well as doing the hard work needed for healthy intimate relationships. It is a relief and a joy to more fully share in the day to day parenting of our daughters. Owning my part in our parenting history, working to have a voice, and pushing for more equitable parenting roles have led to a more satisfying and healthy family life.

Owning my part in less than functional family dynamics has taken me to more than a few dark and painful places. Being honest about and shedding light on them is a critical first step toward healing and growth. Kierkegaard's observation that "Life can only be understood backwards; but it must be lived forwards" comes to mind. I mostly learn in hindsight. A dark and painful experience taught me that as a mom I always need to listen to my gut.

There is a church that our family fully participated in for over seventeen years. This community experienced a number of painful situations throughout these years. Two of the crises involved the revelation of sexual abuse of children. Even writing these words brings up visceral feelings and a gnawing pit deep in my gut. The details of these stories include the abuse of power by those in trusted positions, the victimization of young children and teenage boys, the suicide of a perpetrator, and individual and church blindness accompanied by very dark and secret pain and suffering.

Comfort with the status quo opened the door to insidious evil that thrived in darkness for years but was then jolted into the light.

After the shock and horror subsided in each of these cases, there were gentle invitations to learn and grow as a mom and member of a faith community. It was brutal yet critical that I look in the mirror and seek my own role in letting evil run rampant in a place that I loved. As a mom, I had to confess the "things I had left undone."[12] This included times that people pleasing and fear of rocking the boat trumped the small alarm bells within me warning that things were not quite right. In hindsight and in the process of giving voice to an entire community, we were confronted with the truth that the red flags were right in front of our collective face.

In response to the first revelation of danger for our most vulnerable charges, I joined in with others to research, write, and implement a comprehensive safety and security policy. This was important work, but it did not bring to light an ongoing abusive situation nor prevent the future dark and underground abuse going on in the middle of our community. Only God knows how deep and wide and far this community cancer spread.

In 2008 when the second wave of abuse was revealed, I was personally devastated and felt a deep terror about the wellbeing of my own children, along with that of teenagers that I had known and loved for years. I hope to never ever experience that feeling again. I sank into a black hole of anxiety and depression and had to figure out a way to start slowly clawing my way back up. The fact that all of this was happening in the midst of my church made it all the more complex and destructive. In the midst of this, my growing crisis of faith was nourished. Alongside my body's breakdown and my parental failings, this particular situation was the final shove for me to enter into therapy and get the emotional help I so desperately needed.

Within my church, the only way that seemed appropriate at all to respond to such darkness was to come together with like hearted and minded people and plan a service of sorrow, confession, and lament for any and all victims within and beyond our community. This service involved the lighting of black candles, times of private and public confession, the literal writing on paper and burning of our transgressions, and a chance to express deep grief and lament in response to the darkness in our midst.

Though some in this fellowship were convicted to stay and heal, my husband and I decided to depart this faith community and begin our journey of healing in a different place. I was personally falling apart on so many levels. After wandering around for a time, we landed in a Methodist church. Methodists are really good at imparting and living grace. They also take the safety and security of children very seriously.

A vow that I made after walking this particular journey is to always, always, listen to my gut, particularly around matters involving our children and their fundamental safety and security. This does not mean that I now have license to become an anxious helicopter parent, but I must pay close attention when something in my gut whispers, "this isn't quite right." It is a balance to simultaneously guard against the temptation of living in fear. Though my early religious experience had encouraged "don't rock the boat," "woman, be quiet," and "church people are always trustworthy," I made a vow to myself. Never again.

There are times as we parent our daughters that red flags gently wave and remind me to pay attention. Whether this happens at school, church, or in our neighborhood, my husband and I must stop, consider, and make the best decisions for the situation at hand. We cannot protect our children from all pain and suffering, but we don't ever want to invite these things into their lives through the doors of our own inattention, self-doubt, or discomfort around "rocking the boat" in any particular social interaction. It is quite the delicate balance, but I have learned the hard way that it begins with a commitment to listen to my gut.

As we own our parts, the goal is not to beat ourselves up or to live in a constant state of regret. Honesty and self-awareness are critical, but they are just one step in the direction of healing. One day I had an "aha moment" as I conversed with a trusted family therapist. She had used the term "good enough parent," first coined by Dr. Donald Winnicott, on several occasions. But on this day a light bulb went off inside. Her paraphrased message went something like this. "Even if you could be a perfect parent, and we all know that isn't possible, it is truly best for your child if you are only good enough." A wave of grace washed over me. It is even *better* for my child when I am simply good enough rather than when I waste energy pursuing elusive perfection. This invitation to stop pressuring myself relieved internal tension and a committed pursuit of good enough parenting ensued.

As most thoughtful human beings will acknowledge, true change is hard work and does not happen overnight. But I have been able to change, grow, and reorient my parenting mindset as well as practices. In many ways, the writing of this book is a great big owning of my part.

If I did not take time and energy to closely examine how my very own history, choices, and actions affect those that I love most, I would just bumble along through life unintentionally hurting people all along the way. I would continue to passively choose unhealthy ways to cope and deal, and I would miss out on so much joy. I wholeheartedly believe that beauty can come from ashes.

I have seen it with my own eyes. But this beauty is one that has required a great deal of intention and mindfulness. Unlike the beauty we can all access in nature, this type requires a willingness to labor and commit to a long haul journey. This journey has led me to a number of surprising places.

Reflection

A GRIEF AND A GIFT

During raw encounters with myself as mother in a sacred dance with a hurting child, a turning point was birthed. It sent me on a quest for the many and varied supports and healing paths we need to live as a whole and healthy family. Coming to a place of utter brokenness and vulnerability as mom and human being was the first step in a journey that is both a grief and a gift. I imagine that any parent who navigates life with a child who is different, out of the norm, or has some type of special need is faced with a grief to be felt and a gift to be cherished.

The Grief...

Looking around at other "normal" families, our families are somehow out of step. There is a complexity that though not always seen by the casual observer is still very much a reality. It can show itself in many, many places. We may not be able to fully participate in some of the regular things of life such as certain social events, school activities, or faith communities. Sometimes simple but crucial things like an uninterrupted night of rest are out of reach. Spontaneity is often stifled and desires put aside as we strive to be realistic and constantly mindful of healthy limits and boundaries for both ourselves and our children. And each individual family finds themselves somewhere along this "out of sync" continuum.

The Gift…

Living life with a child that demands we march to the beat of a different drummer is indeed a gift. It is like going to the school of what really matters. It is a crash course in getting over pleasing other people. If embraced, this new perspective quickly leads to a far less judgmental stance toward others. We are acutely aware that we never truly know what is under the behavior of that screaming child in the grocery store or that teenager who is "acting out." We are wise to surrender to a much slower pace of life, which then offers the chance to live in a space of authentic presence and peace. We are entrusted a complex vision of parenthood and what truly matters. We receive the grace of often being able to see beyond the surface into the deep places of life.

With awe, I approach this journey as mommy/mom/mother. Motherhood has wrecked me, formed me, refined me, shaped me, and is an ongoing process that heals both mother and child.

CHAPTER 6

⚬⚬⚬⚬⚬

ATTACHMENT
AND EMOTIONS 101

The best and most beautiful things in the world cannot be seen or even touched—they must be felt with the heart.
Helen Keller

As I continued to travel down a road of both parenting and faith shifts, it became clear that I didn't understand a great deal about feelings and emotions. I realized that when I parented my sons, I considered their expressions of certain feelings as out of bounds. My response to normal human emotions such as anger, frustration, jealousy, and the like was often to label them as disrespectful, disobedient, or shameful. My goal was to prompt each child to shut down strong reactions as soon as possible, or better yet repress them altogether. I needed to reexamine the corporal punishment and timeout/microwave timer strategies that I used with my boys.

Conservative Christian parenting advice often includes the idea that children must obey at first command, and there is a subsequent harsh punishment or isolation if they do not comply. Timeout, corporal punishment, and removal of privileges are touted as appropriate reactions to a child's expression of any "negative" emotion. As I became more fully educated about normal child development, I further questioned the wisdom and truth of the parenting practices I had embraced.

I had to ask and answer a series of important questions: Is there a distinction between "positive" and "negative" emotions? Aren't all feelings a part of being human? Why is any kind of "negative" emotional expression immediately deemed as disrespect and something to be squashed ASAP? Why do I seek to control rather than lovingly teach and mold my children's behaviors? Why do I default to shame and fear tactics to keep my children in line? Sure, kids who are immediately compliant make my life easier, but isn't there something more profound to model and teach these precious souls in my care?

I had hit a wall in parenting my girls. The methods that I had used with my sons were only intensifying problematic behaviors that were happening with our daughters. I was clearly "out of my league." The discipline tools I reached for were like throwing gasoline on a fire. And we were just in the toddler stage of life. I was well aware that there was a long road of parenting ahead.

From a faith perspective, my questions multiplied as well. What is inherently "Christian" about spanking and punishment? Why did I insist that our children meet a standard that I was unable to meet without the gifts of mercy and grace? A major tenet of the Christian faith is that human beings have free will. God does not force us to love, follow, or obey. Though it seems that there are natural consequences that flow out of our choices, God rarely, if ever, flexes big muscles and forces us to walk a certain path. Grace is the overarching story between God and human.

The promise that we can control anyone other than ourselves is quite prevalent as we look around at the voices and practices in much of the parenting advice world. This is a myth. Control by definition requires a level of fear and intimidation. Yes, for a time, we are bigger and stronger than our children, and on some level can force them to do certain things. But did I really want fear-based compliance? As I gradually woke up to the detrimental effects of strict parenting methods, my answer to this question became "no."

One of our daughters regularly reminds me of a difficult truth of our relationship when she says, "You can't *make* me do anything." In former days, I would have preached a mini-sermon and doled out a punishment if a child interacted with me like this. After years of reprogramming my parental brain, I reach for different tools. I give honor to the emotions around such encounters, remind her that in our family we can express anything as long as we are respectful of one another, and then we take the necessary time and intention to work through the core feelings in each tantrum or disagreement.

Sometimes we have to separate for a period of time and then return to the matter at hand. Each of us is granted a "time-out" to process our emotions - my own response is most often to practice deep breathing and get myself in a calmer state. This approach certainly takes more time than doling out a rash and sometimes random consequence, but it also preserves connection and intimate relationship between mother and child. When appropriate, I communicate natural consequences as one portion of a holistic discipline approach.

As hard as it is to admit at times, my daughter's assessment that I can't make her do anything is correct. Her expression of this reality used to send me to a place of great anger, frustration, and then a "digging in" around an attempt to prove her wrong. Though I sometimes still protest internally, I have surrendered to the truth of her words. I now respond with honesty. "You are right. I can't make you do anything. But I hope that you will choose to do this thing that is safest and healthiest for both you and our family." These days, she most often does.

For a while, I lived in the fantasy that I actually controlled my children, their emotions, and their choices. But the raw truth is this: the only one that I can truly manage is myself. There are unhealthy fear based tactics such as brute force (which is only available for a time since they will grow up and become stronger than me), manipulation, and shame that I can attempt to deploy as I navigate the discipline of our kids. The reality is that such methods don't even work that well to control the behavior of many children. Even more importantly, they cause short and long term damage to tender souls as well as to parent-child relationships.

I have decided that I am in this for the long haul. I choose connection and the preservation of a healthy relationship over doing all in my power to get my kids to behave in ways that make *me* most comfortable. When I acknowledge the reality that each of my children is a separate individual soul and not an extension of me or my ego, the level of my comfort around their behavior and choices becomes irrelevant. I am able to see challenges and bumps along the road as opportunities for both me and my child to learn and grow. We are each free to be ourselves and take delight in our differences as well as our shared characteristics and viewpoints. My job is to coach and teach them as they develop and move toward independence.

After years of practicing a parenting paradigm heavy with punishment, I have come to believe that there is a better approach in the training and teaching of a child. A simple, yet far from easy, way to express this change in parenting perspective is a shift from fear to love. In John's first epistle, he said it this way: "There is no fear in love. But perfect love drives out fear, because fear has to do with punishment. The one who fears is not made perfect in love. We love because God first loved us."[13] I, for one, am grateful that God doesn't use a traditional parenting method with me. I need all the grace I can get.

As I delved into changing myself as a mom, there was one concept that kept popping up - attachment. Most anyone who adopts a child must learn about this foundational need for a healthy parent-child relationship. Attachment refers to the interpersonal bond between a parent and a child. Children who begin life in difficult circumstances, such as in chaotic homes, foster care, or an orphanage, always have attachment repair needs. That made sense to me as I prepared to be an adoptive mom. But I was completely unconscious of my own challenges with emotional connection and what I brought to the table as a parent.

John Bowlby and Mary Ainsworth dedicated their lives to exploring what came to be known as Attachment Theory. Attachment Theory asserts that it is critical for an infant to develop a relationship with at least one primary caregiver for the child's successful social and emotional development. This is particularly important for a child as they learn to effectively regulate their feelings. A fundamental tenet of this theory is that infants and children need a reliable caretaker who offers consistent touch and mirroring. Both touch and mirroring are necessary to receive and/or pass along a secure attachment style.

Touch is a concept that we understand without a lot of explanation. Babies need a great deal of tender, physical contact to thrive. Mirroring needs a bit more explanation.

When a mother feeds her baby, about 18 inches from her face, mom and baby gaze into each other's eyes. If the baby coos and smiles after eating, the mother reflects back this satisfaction.[14] If a baby gets distressed, then a mirroring caretaker picks up the baby and reflects the infant's emotion with facial expressions and sometimes words. "Oh, you feel uncomfortable and need to have your diaper changed. I SEE you."

The need for mirroring does not end with infancy. Children, adolescents, and teens also need reliable caretakers to mirror their emotions as they continue to grow and develop. This can only happen when a parent experiences their child as separate and distinct from her/himself. Sometimes parents interact with their children as if they are an extension of themselves. You only have to look as far as a local ball field on a Saturday morning to see this dynamic in action.

As an adoptive mom, I was educated and conscious that my daughters came to our family with complex attachment needs. But as a mother, I was not aware of the dysfunctions on my side of the attachment dance that had already played out with each of my five children. I was not prepared for the revelation of my very own adult attachment challenges as a wife, mom, and person navigating the world. Something that resided in an unconscious place was about to come into the light.

I remember sitting at an Empowered to Connect conference for adoptive parents and hearing the story of a mom who came face-to-face with this reality in her own life. As she got professional help with parenting her adopted child, she realized that her attachment deficiencies affected parent-child interactions even as she mothered her older biological child. As I sat in the chair listening to her story, I experienced a lightning bolt of "me too" followed by a kick in the gut feeling. On that day, I more fully realized that my ignorance about my own attachment challenges had on some level affected all of my children. I had not mirrored them well.

I have heard it said that even though children are great recorders of events, they are terrible interpreters.[15] As I look back on my own early life, I see the wisdom in this. Throughout my childhood, my mom suffered a series of health challenges. As a child, I had no way to make sense of some of the dynamics within my home. I remember one day finding my mother in great pain. I felt terrified that she might die, and I desperately wished that someone would help me figure out what to do about this situation. My parents held to a belief that "we should not burden our children with adult matters." There was little follow up, explanation, or communication about my mom's health issues, so I was left to interpret (most often quite incorrectly) complicated feelings and circumstances alone. No one mirrored my confused and painful emotions during these times.

There also are family tales of my parents leaving me in my crib to "cry it out." Dr. Spock encouraged a generation of parents to employ this strategy when infants had sleep issues. Though it depends on the circumstances, duration, and frequency of such crying, this parenting strategy can affect an infant's ability to securely attach emotionally to a parent. As a child and teenager, I spent a great deal of time banished to my room after times when I expressed my emotions in a loud fashion. I have a distinct memory of "acting up" in church during my elementary years. My father marched me to the car, spanked me, and then left me there to sit until church was over. I remember feeling great frustration and rage during such times.

As a child, I was not mirrored well. My very normal human emotions were not named or honored. Sometimes they were punished. Therefore, I struggled to express my feelings in healthy ways. I experienced a lot of anger and frustration. As the older of two children, I felt pressure to conform to my parents' wishes and beliefs. When I did not do so, I often wondered if I disappointed them. As I entered adulthood, I experienced tremendous tension as I sometimes tried to please them and other times wanted to rebel and fight against their expectations. This must have been confusing for them.

I imagine that my parents were also not mirrored well, but that is their story to tell. No one in my family set out to intentionally hurt me. My parents were doing the best that they knew to do within the reality of their lives. Each of my parents, in their own way, has communicated this to me. I wholeheartedly believe and forgive them. I have asked my sons to forgive me for my emotional deficiencies in their childhoods. They have.

For many of us who have difficulties feeling emotionally secure in close relationships, we tend to play this out with our first-born child. Because I am a first born, I pay particular attention to this role in family. I breastfed my first son for a year and spent a great deal of time locked in mutual gaze (I am grateful that smartphones were not on the scene in my earliest mom years!) But as he became a toddler, I struggled to mirror him well. I think back to the earlier story of chasing him with a spanking stick as I nursed his baby brother. Not only did that interfere with my infant's attachment, but also that of my toddler. My two-year old boy was expressing his autonomy and separateness from me, but I saw him as an extension of myself. I treated his developmentally appropriate behavior as something to be suppressed. Rather than mirror his emotions and delight in his uniqueness, I tried to get him to mold to my expectations.

I imagine that it is not always the first born that ends up in this dynamic, but they are so often the "guinea pig." So many of my hopes and dreams were forced onto this one individual child. In our family, our second born was so interestingly different from my husband and me that we were more able to delight in him. Our firstborn son is like me in many ways, and maybe that played into my blindness around these issues. I experienced him as an extension of myself rather than a separate, individual soul.

Not only did my struggles with healthy emotional expression affect mother-child interactions, it also bled over into other relationships. My particular adult attachment style played out in this way: though I felt worthy of love, I did not have confidence that those in close relationship would in fact meet my needs. I often found myself doubting that my husband truly loved me. It could be as petty and off base as the thought, "he won't be willing to clean up the kitchen even if I ask him." But it also colored much deeper aspects of our relationship. I was reluctant to bring up concerns in various facets of our marriage. "My voice doesn't matter, and he won't change anyway," was the lie I often told myself. Of course this affected our relationship on many different levels.

Often, the jobs that we choose or the life paths we follow are informed by an unconscious desire to heal our attachment challenges. My choice to adopt children falls into this category. My journey as an adoptive mom both revealed my deficiencies as well as offered the opportunity for tremendous healing in figuring out how to experience emotionally secure relationships.

When I was faced with the emotional needs of children who had experienced trauma, I reached into my parenting toolbox and came up empty handed. Over a now twelve-year journey, I have moved toward healthy and secure attachment with those I am in close relationship. Each step that I took toward self-care, becoming fully human, and owning my part within our family led to both physical and emotional healing for myself as well as our family. On this deep matter of attachment, there has been a slow and steady march toward wholeness. It required looking at myself honestly, finding ways to have a voice, and offering compassion to my family and myself. For me, the most direct way to healing has been within an ongoing supportive relationship with a therapist.

Thankfully, there is a redemptive message on the matter of healthy emotional development. If we realize that we have struggles in this area, there is something that we can work toward - it is a place of grace called "earned or evolved secure attachment."[16] In other words, our emotional health can shift. We can experience life believing that we are worthy of love as well as learn to trust the love of those with whom we are intimately connected. We can change. Our brokenness can be redeemed.

It seems paradoxical that a place of grace involves earning something. But once I made a commitment to take action and make changes, grace showed up. As I opened up to mental health supports as an individual and as a mom, this area of my life began to heal. Practicing yoga, mindfulness, and meditation also played a key role in these shifts. I learned to identify and sit with various feelings. I began to understand that my strong emotions would not overwhelm me. I grew in the ability to tolerate and empathize with the emotions of others.

I started to share my insecurities with my husband as well as get curious about what he was thinking and feeling. In earlier days, I often acted as if I could read his mind as I assigned motives and thoughts to him through my own filter. I found out that most of the time, I was a terrible mind reader!

I began to ask my husband and children to help with all of the many tasks required to manage a home and family. When we get together in large family settings or vacations, we now literally prepare spreadsheets of shared responsibilities. Everyone pitches in to help with cooking, cleaning, arranging outings, and all of the details surrounding such gatherings. My husband and I do not have to carry so much of the physical burden around the logistics of our family get-togethers. I can ask for help when I need it. Special connections are formed and solidified among various family members as we work, cook, and clean side by side.

In other words, my family mirrored my emotions and needs. They SAW me. I could only receive this gift after I began to deeply know that I was worthy of such support. When I began to speak up and ask for what I wanted, they began paying attention to my own unique needs and then meeting them. This began within the wife/husband relationship and then extended out into our family.

When I was no longer in a place of feeling ignored, inadequate, or overwhelmed, I was in a healthier position to be a parent to my daughters who desperately needed me to be fully present for them. When I finally faced my attachment needs, I was able to love my family freely without reservation. The healthier I got, the healthier were those around me.

After a great deal of hard work and intention, I now experience secure attachments with my husband as well as my children. I feel both worthy of love as well as capable of receiving the support and love that I need. I trust that those that I am in intimate relationship with are willing and able to love and help me. This has required a large mind and heart transition that has happened over many years and with a great deal of support and mindfulness. My attachment challenges have been transformed. Because of this particular transformation, I am now able to truly experience the abundant life that I heard so much about in my religious tradition. I now realize the gift of true freedom.

One autumn, on a beautiful, sunny, North Carolina day, I sat on the front porch with my friend Donna. Somehow, the conversation made its way around to the topic of attachment and the family systems we had each experienced. I paraphrase Donna's words on that day: "If I admit that I have challenges in developing trust and making emotional connections in my most important relationships, then I am admitting that there is something fundamentally deficient about me." Her words haunted and challenged me as they pinged back and forth between heart and head. I took this exchange to my therapist, and her wise response was, "To know our deficiencies is incredibly freeing." Jesus said it this way, "You will know the truth, and the truth will set you free."[17]

I have experienced the truth of this wisdom. As I faced my own deficiencies in the area of attachment, it was a first step on a pathway toward emotional healing. As long as I lived in a place of denial, I mindlessly lived and related to others from a place of ignorance and fear. But as I accepted my personal limitations, I was then free to make changes and live in healthier relationships within my family. Rather than becoming defensive and hurt when my husband brings up delicate or problematic dynamics in our relationship, I am now able to hear him and talk about it. Instead of carrying anger toward my parents over things that I wish had been different, I can now see things from their perspective and enjoy the relationship that we have. I am now able to offer compassion to myself as a young inexperienced mom. Each of us was doing the best we knew to do at the time. And as I became more self-aware, I could choose to live differently.

As I began addressing my need for healthier emotional expression and connections within intimate relationships, a good place to begin to relearn and practice was in the area of feelings. Very soon I was offered various opportunities to become a student in the classroom of life. "Wilson Emotions 101" was the course offered. I had a lot to learn. The ongoing invitation to understand my own emotions as well as the realization of the importance of mirroring the feelings of my children provided opportunities for this crash course.

I was getting ready to learn how to detect both my own emotional shifts and the emotional states of my children. One day as I sat in the familiar waiting room of a family therapist, a thin forty-eight paged book caught my eye. I picked up *What Am I Feeling?* and began to leaf through it. Its message pulled me in immediately and by the end of that forty-five minute wait, it literally changed my life.

Even though I was a psychology major in college, I had not made the connection that my shortcomings around the topic of feelings was greatly affecting my parenting style and thus the emotional lives of my children. During my own childhood and beyond, I learned that certain feelings were most often something to be either disapproved of or dismissed. As a child and teenager, I spent a great deal of time in my room for "backtalk" or disrespect. As a young mom, faced with a range of big and loud emotional expressions by my children, I often did not know what to do, beyond trying to make it stop. My kids also spent time isolated in their rooms. I came up short in teaching my children how to deal with strong feelings.

"What Am I Feeling?" proved to be the Emotions 101 course that I as mom was lacking. In this book, Dr. John Gottman describes four different parenting styles. "The dismissing style" is one in which a parent pushes away emotions deemed negative. "It's not that bad. You are fine. There is no reason for you to feel so unhappy."

"The disapproving style" shows up when "bad" emotions are punished, criticized, or shamed. "There is no reason for you to feel sad/angry/jealous. If you don't stop crying, you are going to be in trouble."

"The laissez-faire style" is when a parent encourages a child to let all of their feelings out, but there are no boundaries around the accompanying behavior. "However you feel and want to express that is fine with me. Go ahead and let all your feelings out."

The fourth and healthiest is "the emotion coaching style" which empathizes with any feeling expressed and then helps a child figure out how to self-regulate. "I understand that you feel angry, and I have felt that way as well. It is not ok to kick someone when you are feeling this way. Let's figure out a way for you to deal with this feeling."[18]

I mostly saw my own parenting style reflected in the dismissive and disapproving categories. Acknowledging this led to feelings of regret and shame, but grace and gentleness also showed up. Grateful for a way forward, I committed to pursue the role of emotion coach. The expression of "negative" emotions became fertile ground to both learn and teach that we all feel a variety of feelings. "There's no such thing as a 'bad' emotion. It's how we handle our emotions that matters."[19] There would be many moments and situations in days ahead when I had to implement the important task of mirroring my kids, put on my coaching hat, and get to work. One particular Sunday morning, I was given the chance to practice my growing mirroring skills with our daughter.

She had longed for, dreamed of, and planned how to make it happen for months. It had lots of pockets, pouches, and zippers. It was one of her favorite colors, camouflage green. This Bible cover was "it." Spotted at the Sunday school Bible bucks store, this cover required a long process of showing up and doing various activities to earn the purchasing power for this much-desired item. Bible buck deals and trades with her sister had been made, broken, and renegotiated, delaying the procurement of this yearned for object. She worked extra hard to secure the needed bucks for the deal.

Sunday was the day. She had enough to purchase the cover as well as five extra bucks to buy canned goods to donate to those in need of food. She counted and recounted and had a plan. As we got ready to leave the house, she dropped hints and obviously couldn't wait to get in the car and head to church. Running ahead, she got into line, anxious to make this long awaited, in the life of a nine year old, purchase.

As I came up a minute or so later, I could read the distress on her face. Holding back tears, she said, "It's gone." Someone a bit ahead of her in line had scored this treasured item. I reached out to comfort her and with body language and words, she pushed me away. My heart hurt for her as I felt the big drop of disappointment alongside her. When she emotionally pushed back, my immediate response was to just walk away in my own rejected state, a pattern left over from my attachment challenges. But as I took a few steps down the hall, a still small voice whispered, "Don't walk away. Give this a little time." I took a deep breath, whispered to her that I would be waiting on a couch toward the end of the line, and extended an invitation to please come see me after she made it through the line. This small amount of time and space allowed each of us to slightly settle our strong immediate emotional responses to the situation.

Though this incident might seem small and relatively insignificant from an adult viewpoint, it mattered greatly to my daughter. It is always a challenge to stand by and respond in healthy ways when our children face varying shades of adversity. Some of us have a "go to" of dismissing or disapproving of the feelings involved in such events and somehow communicate to our children a "get over it, this is not a big deal, you will be fine" message. Others of us tend to want to shield and protect our children from such strong feelings and tend to rush in and save our children from any and all discomfort. To help our kids move toward healthy ways of dealing with strong emotions requires something in the middle. This was a great opportunity for me to step into the role of an emotion coach. "Tell me how you feel. I understand that feeling and have felt that way as well. Let's figure out together healthy ways to express your emotions and deal with the situation."

On that Sunday when my sweet girl joined me on the couch, I did my best to be a coach. I shared her disappointment and celebrated that she stayed in line and purchased the altruistic five cans of food for someone who is hungry despite her big disappointment. There was a big tug of war internally as I considered going to the person in charge of the Bible bucks store, telling her the story, and trying to make it all better with a replacement cover. But I also knew this could be an important learning experience for mom and daughter. I want to empower my children to speak up when they have desires and disappointments. Maybe this was one of those times. I felt conflicted. I honestly don't think there is a "right or wrong" approach here, but it was a chance to dialogue and learn for both of us. On that day I decided I would not intervene but would support. My daughter knew that I would be by her side as coach if she decided to communicate her wish, but this time I was not going to try and fix it for her.

That afternoon, I was relaxing and reading through Brené Brown's book *Daring Greatly*, and the chapter on Wholehearted Parenting.[20] A brief definition of Wholehearted is someone who is resilient to shame, believes in her worthiness, and is emotionally healthy. Brown is a vulnerability researcher and discovered something that caught my attention in light of my morning experience. "What do parents experience as the most vulnerable and bravest thing that they do in their efforts to raise Wholehearted children?. . . . letting their children struggle and experience adversity."[21] As coach mom, I was grateful for confirmation on that day. As hard as it is to do sometimes, letting my child feel, deal with, and experience adversity has great value. Each situation is different, but in general, children need a coach rather than a feelings denier or a fixer. They need a parent that they feel securely attached to who can mirror their feelings. We as parents need to be present in the midst of difficult emotions and learn to tolerate our own discomfort as we work to guide and support. As I became more mindful of such things, the opportunities to respond to my children from a place of healthy attachment continued to roll out before me.

Though I, as a mom, often feel pressure to be the fixer of all things problematic for my children, it is much healthier if I can take on the role of a reflector. When the temptation to jump in and save my kids from all hardship arises, there is also an invitation to walk alongside and serve as a support and a coach.

At one point, one of our daughters was over thinking and really struggling to do a task that was important for her to accomplish. Something that typically takes about one to two minutes to do was literally taking hours because of debilitating anxiety. Walking through this experience together took an emotional toll on her and me. But in reality, this was fertile ground for me to sit still in an uncomfortable place and learn to tolerate both my own and her emotions through this process. It was also instructive for a child who tends to stuff and deny feelings to practice expressing them.

I am learning that the more mindful and honest that I am about my feelings, the more I can give the same gift to my children. When I rush to reassure my child when he is in distress, this sends a message that I can't tolerate whatever is being expressed. My desire to dismiss emotions with a quick "you'll be fine" teaches my child that feelings are not acceptable. Through the heart and eyes of a child, such a response can be translated into "I am not acceptable." Repeating this over and over will lead to children who become adults that deny, repress, and shove aside strong feelings.

There is a sweet spot between dismissing and over engaging with our children in times of distress. We each bring our own story and challenges to the table of guiding our children through emotional turmoil. In my early days of waking up to my role in the emotional family dynamic, my personal comfort zone was stretched.

When someone I love expresses a disappointment, frustration, or failing, often my initial response is to get the mental wheels turning on what exactly I can offer to "fix" the problem. What words of wisdom or advice can I come up with to help them come to a more peaceful place? Like some kind of savior or super hero, how can I swoop in and make it all better? I respond this way as a result of my particular attachment challenges, assuming that no one else is going to address a problem if I don't take charge.

In reality, this "I must fix it" response comes from a place where my own anxiety around normal human emotional expression rises. It sometimes reveals a selfish focus on how I may appear as mom/wife/person, and other times exposes a limited tolerance for seeing someone I love in an uncomfortable place. No matter the source, my spouting off in such a moment is not helpful, in any way, for anyone. It only leads to greater frustration for the child I am trying to "fix" and leads them to feel "mom just doesn't understand me." And thus attachment challenges are passed from parent to child. It requires a great deal of intention and practice to change such patterns, but it can be done.

Along my journey toward healthier attachment with my loved ones and greater awareness of my emotions, one January I chose a meditation focus to practice throughout the next 365 days. For all of 2015 my mantra became "reflect, don't fix." It was something I practiced over and over again. While doing yoga or sitting in silent meditation, I would breathe in "reflect" and breathe out "don't fix." When confronted with an actual fix it temptation, before speaking, I did the same. I changed several account passwords to "reflect, don't fix." Everything that I could do to saturate my heart and mind with this thought was helpful.

Reflect has a twofold meaning. When confronted with a situation, stop and reflect before speaking. In addition, when in the presence of another's frustration, offer words of reflection and empathy rather than suggestions on how to make it all better. In other words, mirror the other person.

As is almost always the case, when I set my mind and heart toward a specific intent, situations arise to allow me to practice. One of our girls is passionate, opinionated, and always willing to speak up about injustice. I love these things about her. Giving voice to such a tender and fiery heart is critical, and coaching her on how to present such passion in a way that others can hear and receive is sometimes a challenge. She has written the president, governor, county commissioners, and police department expressing her myriad concerns and ideas.

During her fifth grade school year, she decided to write to a few of the teachers at her school about a perceived injustice around recess time. I was vaguely aware that she was rather secretively working on this and offered just two thoughts as she worked through her words. "Be respectful and you need to sign your name." I did not read the letters.

The next day as she plopped in the car after her day at school, she muttered, "Well that didn't go so well." In follow up, it became clear that one of the adult letter recipients was upset and felt unjustly accused. As a bit of backstory, as a child and sometimes even as an adult, I would almost rather curl up and die than be confronted by an angry authority figure. My issue.

This situation offered up a chance to practice my 2015 focus. I literally took a deep breath, breathed in "reflect" and then out "don't fix." The predominant voice in my head said, "Put your own issues and ego aside. This is a tremendous learning opportunity for your daughter." An incredibly mature and fruitful conversation ensued. A few of the lessons that we discussed were: when we confront people, we need to be ready and able to receive their emotions; it is important to make sure we have our facts straight before we challenge another; other people may have things going on in their lives that lead to an over response that has nothing to do with us; we should not apologize if we don't truly mean it, but if there are honest heartfelt apologies to be made, it can help restore a relationship.

I did not need to jump in and try to fix this on any level. Shared words of reflection were enough. This is not to say that

I never intervene on behalf of my children. At times, I do. But as they get older, the goal is to empower them to handle situations of conflict. I try to first reflect their feelings and concerns, and then ask permission to offer any advice. I am learning to be ok when my offer is rejected. As a mom, I prefer the role of coach rather than savior or fixer. The bottom line truth is that I have no power to fix or save. But I can work to model and live a life of healthy emotional expression. Then, the opportunity for attachment healing within myself and my child is possible. This is true even as I interact with my grown children.

So many of the lessons that I learned in the school of "Emotions 101" didn't happen until my sons were practically grown and gone from our home. Though many times I wished for a do-over with them, obviously that is not possible. But there are healing pathways within relationships, and it is never too late to do my part to make amends. I agree with Maya Angelou who said, "Do the best you can until you know better. Then when you know better, do better." Certainly, pieces of my own emotional challenges passed onto my sons in one form or another. I am not able to go back and re-parent them. But I do have the opportunity to own my part in this area and move forward in the light of such knowledge. The way forward with each of my sons has looked different and unique to each mother-son relationship.

Shortly after I read the paradigm shifting "*What Am I Feeling?*" book, I ordered three copies with the intent to share them with my boys if and when they became fathers. Recently, through conversation and contemplation, I decided to go ahead and address head-on my own deficiencies as their mother by sending them a package. This package contained a heartfelt letter expressing my feelings toward them, my personal challenges as a mom, and my hope that they will make different choices if they choose to parent. Now it is up to them.

A few summers ago, when my older daughter was between the sixth and seventh grades, we had about five days together in our home. Mark and our youngest child traveled to visit family in Chicago. I invited my girl to read the "daughter half" of the book *Mothering and Daughtering: Keeping Your Bond Strong Through the Teenage Years* by Eliza and Sil Reynolds. This child is an introvert, loves to read, and delights in quiet time alone. She is a quiet soul whose voice often gets drowned out by those around her. Though I offered that we could head to the beach or mountains to discuss this book, she chose to stay home. We had time and space to connect and enjoy each other on a deeper level than is afforded during the everydays of life. It was a special time that I will always remember.

Though she rolled her eyes and wasn't too sure about discussing this book together, she complied. Interspersed around the discussion times, we did things we enjoy both separately and together. We made great memories and shared deep emotions, as we laughed and connected in significant ways. *Mothering and Daughtering* provided a structure and springboard for deeper communication. She got to tell me what I am doing well and where I can improve. I shared with her stories of my growing up days and relationships. We binge watched "Once Upon a Time," cooked and ate delicious food together, got green and purple pedicures, and talked about the specific ways that the two of us can stay connected in days and years to come.

We took a day trip to a nearby city, hung out with people we love, and then she indulged her old mama as we together went to see the show "Three acts, two dancers, one radio host." Ira Glass of *This American Life* is one of my favorite radio personalities, and seeing him up close and in person was a delight. Though it wasn't her favorite evening out, she made me laugh out loud with her reflections afterward. "I got the references that were from *my* century. I think it was intended for people born in the 1900's." She did have a point – we were born in different centuries.

On the third day into our retreat, my daughter came down one morning singing and humming "The Best Day" by Taylor Swift. This is my very favorite Swift song. It is about a mom and her daughter, and my girls know that when I hear it, I am likely to tear up. My heart swelled, and I just soaked in her musical gift to me without saying a word.

I blogged about this magical five-day retreat, and then a few days later, I received this text from a dear friend: "I've spent years trying to get over my sense that who I am is profoundly disappointing to my mom. What fun it is to read about a mom seeing her girls as individuals, and working to foster a deep relationship with them. Keep it up!!" This friend has a beautiful soul, and it is hard for me to imagine who it is that her mother wishes that she had become.

As my daughter and I read the *Mothering and Daughtering* book, I was reminded of the importance of mirroring our children throughout their lives. The authors said it this way, "Mirroring your daughter [or son] is seeing her for who she is and reflecting back to her who you see, without judgment or agenda... [this] communicates, 'I see you, and I deeply value who you are and who you are becoming'."[22]

What brand new parent holding a newborn baby does not have hopes and dreams of who this fragile miracle in their arms will grow up to be? And in the blink of an eye, this baby becomes a toddler who makes it known that they also have a will and desire of their very own, separate from that of the parent. This can be the beginning of a beautiful dance of reflection and guidance or a battle cry that can lead to civil war for years to come. It all depends upon the stance of the parent. I have participated in both.

Carl Jung once said, "The greatest burden a child must bear is the unlived life of the parent." I would add to this statement "or a parent's burning desire for a repeat performance." My greatest moments of heartbreak as mom have come when something that is dear to me has been rejected by one of my children. When this happens, I need to acknowledge the pain, grieve the loss, and then make peace within myself.

I believe that the all too familiar adolescent cry of "you just don't get me/understand me" is a deep shout out to the parental heart to "please just see me for who I am and be delighted in who I am becoming even though, and especially when, I walk a path different from one that you, my parent, might choose." Does this mean that we will not correct, teach, and pass along our values? No. But it does mean that we will be attuned and in tune with who our children are at their very core – their soul – and encourage them to become their truest selves.

For me, fear is almost always one of the hurdles in the way of accepting my children just as they are at any given time. At times like these, I remember the words, "there is no fear in love." My children will walk paths and make decisions that displease or deeply concern me. The less I try to control that and the more that I can acknowledge the fear and make wide the space inside of me for love and grace, the more effectively I can be a mirror to them as they figure it all out. When the fear and attempts to control are at bay, there is much more room for joy and delight as we live life as family.

Reflection

When we adopted our first daughter, our sons were a senior and freshman in high school and a seventh grader smack in the center of middle school. For a variety of reasons, we always knew that we would prefer to adopt two children. There was solid parental and family discussion and reasoning behind this decision. But we were in quite a hurry. A mere thirteen months later, we added a second daughter to our family. I have absolutely no regrets that this spunky and incredible girl entered our family. Our family needed this self-proclaimed "grand finale." We love her dearly. She has changed each one of us for the better.

Yet, there was a price paid by our sons. They navigated critical years without parents who had the time and energy to regularly coach and come alongside. This was especially true for our youngest son. During these days, a friend close to this son said to me, "I think he feels ignored and is struggling since you adopted the girls. He needs more attention." I brushed it off and felt defensive.

Recently, I publicly wrote something about our sons in reference to their many summers spent on our neighborhood swim and tennis teams. "Our boys were more of the coach's award type kids than MVP winners." Our youngest boy, now man, gently and privately sent me a message that he had in fact won MVP in tennis twice during his high school years. I truly have absolutely no recollection of that fact.

I responded to my son with honest words. "I was fairly checked out during your high school years. I am sorry about that." After he offered forgiveness and a gracious understanding that I was doing what I had to do during that period of our family's life, I responded, "I truly am sorry that you paid a price though I know you are gracious and forgiving. We can talk about this sometime…" Text messages aren't the best avenue for such intimate conversation.

I recounted this story to my friend Liisa, and she offered true and gracious words. "At least you are talking about it now." Way down in the depths of my heart, I believe that just about every human being is doing the best that they can on any given day. The same applies to me as mom.

Many things will happen along the parenthood journey that disrupt or affect the kind of parenting we hope to practice. Some we have a hand in choosing and some sneak up and blindside us. Denial and silence around such things often multiply the pain, but speaking the truth of them in love leads to healing. As long as there is breath, it is never too late to experience the balm of forgiveness that comes when we live into the place of "at least you are talking about it now."

CHAPTER 7

⟨⟨⟨⟨⟨⟨⟩

TREASURES OF DARKNESS

Along with the joy of parenthood, with every child comes a piercing vulnerability. It is at once sublime and terrifying.
David Sheff, in *Beautiful Boy*

There is a truth of being human that is often difficult to acknowledge and accept. Actress and writer Emma Thompson said it like this: "It's unfortunate, and I really wish I wouldn't have to say this, but I really like human beings who have suffered. They're kinder." Most of us who are willing to be honest about our own darkest hours as well as let into our hearts the pain and suffering of others will come to agree with this sentiment. Suffering softens, if we allow it to do so.

As a parent, I have experienced situations with my children that cloud and shadow our family life as well as times in which I felt plunged into darkness. Given a choice, I would avoid almost all pain and suffering. And as a mom, I would rarely if ever choose for my child to experience hardship, pain, sorrow, or even discomfort. Many of us work hard to shield, avoid, and prevent even an inkling of distress from entering the lives of our children. Is this a healthy pursuit?

I recently sat in a room full of middle school parents as we learned of an impending field trip scheduled for our twelve and thirteen year olds. Information was shared that they would be traveling to a site where they would experience a 24-hour simulation of various global and rural cultures. Each simulation would include a level of hunger and poverty. As the plans were revealed, there was squirming and a level of discomfort in the room, and then one mom raised her hand. "I guess we are all a little uncomfortable with the idea of our children being uncomfortable, but it will be good for them. Right?"

Looking at the big picture, we all can agree on some level with the statement made by the slightly unsure middle school mom, though we rarely choose the uncomfortable for ourselves or for our kids. But if we live long enough, life will happen and pain and suffering will roll into our families. Beloved grandparents and pets die. People we love get sick. Challenging friendships and hurtful words come along. And sometimes life changing tragedies visit those we love most.

In the childhood ditty "going on a bear hunt," there is wisdom. "Can't go over it, can't go under it, gotta go through it." Our children will experience heartache, heartbreak, and many different facets of pain and suffering. There is no sensible way to shelter them from much of this reality. I have learned that rather than try to keep them in a protective bubble, it is best to come alongside, give honor and space to their pain and suffering, and walk right through it together. They need guidance, a safe place to express any and all feelings, and to always know that "come what may, mom and dad are right by my side."

On the topic of life's challenges, there are varying degrees and flavors of such experiences. Sometimes heartaches weave in and out of the everyday moments in life. School, home, church, and neighborhoods are all fertile ground to learn of the satisfactions and disappointments that are an integral part of relationships. After mothering three sons, I realize that there is a different slant as I support my daughters in navigating the world of friendships.

I know that girls can be mean. I started the book *Queen Bees and Wannabes* a few years ago but found it so depressing that I couldn't get past the first few chapters. We have the American Girl books on friendships and have read them. I had heard from seasoned moms that sometime during the later elementary years, the mean girl thing really heats up. The truth is that back in my own coming of age days, I was at times both a mean girl and a mean girl target.

I have raised three sons. They certainly had their share of disagreements and squabbles, but the male way of dealing with things is most often quite direct and efficient. A kick, a punch, and then usually approximately two minutes later, back to the task at hand, and all are still friends. It is most often over and done just like that.

There are historical and understandable reasons that females are unaccustomed to communicating in an assertive and direct voice. We have learned through the generations to try and get the things we want by using more indirect routes. Sometimes passive-aggressive means, as well as charm and manipulation, have served us well in a male-centric society. Finding our healthy, assertive voice is a challenge.

As a mom of girls, one thing I wasn't prepared for was the heart drop I feel when my own daughter is the victim of girl snarkiness. All of the girls involved in this particular story are talented and often kind-hearted kids. There is mean girl potential within us all.

It was a beautiful day, and there was a great deal of excitement in the air over a school sponsored 5K race. My daughter had attended practices for this event and was quite certain that she had her running buddies all lined up. On race day, the young runners gathered and made last minute plans with friends to run alongside each other. Three times I watched my daughter reach out to another, and three times she was rejected on some level. After each rejection, her shoulders slumped and her face was crestfallen. It was quite painful to watch, from afar and up close. I first felt a bit paralyzed. In late elementary school, we were well past the point where it is acceptable for mom to intervene and make it all ok. Yet I needed to acknowledge the hurt she was experiencing. I took a deep breath, shot up a prayer, and then did the best I could. My girl's body language and unwillingness to engage in conversation around what was happening communicated to me that I as mom was going to have to tolerate and deal with my own feelings. She would figure this out.

Grace entered the scene on this day as two beloved teachers came across our path. Maybe they saw the panic in my eyes or maybe the hurt and confusion in the eyes of my daughter. They excitedly invited her to run with them and off they went together. I decompressed, felt my heart rise up, thanked God for teachers, and waited peacefully and expectantly for her to run across the finish line. She ran fast and hard, spurred on by these two people she loves, and crossed the finish line well ahead of most of her peers, including two that had hurt her feelings. Ok, now I'm being snarky.

There is still so much for each of us to learn as both daughter and mom. At the end of this run, a dear friend and mom of a grown daughter reminded me of how resourceful my girls are and that these things will happen along the way. My heart would like to shield them from all meanness as instigator or recipient, but my mind knows that is neither possible nor healthy. These are times that invite each of us to learn and grow. I know that on any given day, my girls, just like their mom, can land on either side of the mean girl equation. I've seen evidence of both. On this race day a little time needed to pass before my daughter was ready to engage me in what happened and how she felt. My job was to listen for all spoken and unspoken signals and wait for a time when she was able to put voice to her own feelings. That happened as we drove home from the race.

My goal is to raise daughters who are kind and compassionate and can process and handle the meanness of others in healthy ways. The only way to get there is through practice and living into days like this day. My role is not to interfere or fix or deny but to listen, receive their feelings, and sometimes offer encouragement as they grow and mature and figure it all out.

Sometimes the heartbreak and suffering that enter our lives as parent are much more painful and challenging than the everyday setbacks that happen along the way. The stakes are much higher. When someone we love is in severe crisis or a life-threatening situation, our response is often to beg God for a miracle. Especially when that someone is our child.

I've walked through life long enough to observe and experience that miracles do indeed happen. But the why, how, and whens of such supernatural events are a complete mystery. It seems to me that it is dangerous and detrimental on so many levels to believe that if we believe and pray in just the right way, with just the right posture, and get just the right people to join in, we can be assured of the miracle we so desire. My earliest conservative religion did not prepare me for the very real nuances and complexities around this topic.

In recent years, I have observed people of great faith thrust into fighting life-threatening battles alongside their beloved sons and daughters. On more than one occasion, the final outcome has been every parent's deepest vulnerability and fear – the death of a child. I have also witnessed events of great and unexpected healing in the lives of others. It is a rare event, yet it does happen against the predictions of scientific, medical, and human reason. My heart mourns with those who have experienced great pain and loss and rejoices with those who have experienced extraordinary healing and mercy. Yet I find this "miracle territory" to be a place of confusion and doubt. A delicate balance is necessary to make any sense of it all within my heart, soul, and mind. As a person comfortable asking the question "why?" this particular matter leads to great unsettling doubts.

When there is a big miracle in the midst of a community, I wonder how those who didn't get one in their hour of desperate pleas and prayers process this. Are they angry and resentful? Are they able to rejoice with those who rejoice, or is it just too painful at times? Do they have a safe place to express their deepest doubts and questions? Making peace with a God who can intervene, but doesn't, is tough work.

And for those I know who have received their heart's desire and their particular prayer for a miracle became a reality, what does that feel like? Though there is much gratitude and joy, is it uncomfortable in any way – something akin to survivor's guilt?

These are big questions, and there are no trite and easy answers. One thing that I have observed is that those who come through a devastating loss with faith intact also demonstrate the miraculous, often in the most profound ways. I take great comfort in the real life stories of those whose heart desire met a resounding "no" and yet they still trust God and experience joy. In Isaiah, God states, "For my thoughts are not your thoughts neither are your ways my ways."[23] Humbling and for a sometimes rebel like me, not too satisfying at times.

As a mom, I desire to become more at peace with the mystery of God's action and sometimes seeming inaction within our family stories. I imagine that embracing the questions of faith and doubt and all that is God will be happening until the day that I depart this life. For many years, I debated the mystery of the miracle as an observer – sometimes from afar and at other times from a closer perspective. Then one day, I had a front row seat. It was terrifying.

It was 2014 during a string of October 70-degree North Carolina blue sky days, just a few months after we moved into a new home. The weather beckoned and called out to our older daughter and led her to time spent alone in her new backyard. On one such day, I realized that she had climbed way up into a tree in the corner of our yard. The tug of war between "protective mommy" and "encourage the risk taking mom" flitted through my mind as she excitedly shared her adventure with me. There was a nest way up high. She was so excited. The "adventure loving, put my fears aside mom" won out. The "be careful" mom voice was quelled. In hindsight, a more full integration of the two would have been appropriate.

On Friday night, good friends arrived at our home to enjoy our new place, and our four girls excitedly ran around to explore. We were midway through an adult home tour when I heard the voice of our younger girl. It was frantic and of an unusual pitch. Her sister had fallen from a tree. "Come now!" I ran to the tree and what I saw almost stopped my heart. My tiny sixty-pound girl lay flat on the ground. I know that some of my auto pilot response was shock, but I also in that moment knew deep in my soul that undivided and true presence with my child was critical. Everything else must fall away.

I have practiced and practiced symbolically holding my children in the palm of my hands and letting them go to God. As I knelt down beside my precious, barely conscious girl, my heart and hands let go. I was full of terror, but the raw truth was this was a situation over which I had absolutely no control.

In that moment I knew in a way I've never known before that I must remain present for my girl and that there were no guarantees whatsoever about how this particular story would unfold. It was a severe surrender.

Very soon the EMS team arrived, and they asked lots and lots of questions of my daughter and of me. She was extremely confused, but she was talking and conscious on some level. "Altered state" is how they described it. How far up was she? I literally could not make myself look up to the height of the nest that she excitedly told me about just a day or two before. After an inspection of the magnolia tree and conversations with the three 9 to 11 year old witnesses to the fall, we learned that she was about 15 feet high when the branch snapped. The nest she shared with me was located at least double that height in the same tree. The EMS team kept saying she fell 15-20 feet. I now believe that they knew that a 30-40 foot drop would have played out in a much different way.

The EMS team was amazing. As we loaded up into the ambulance, the driver spoke incredibly gentle and merciful words to me. "Mom, we don't see anything too critical at this point, but we are going to use lights and sirens to get there ASAP." "PLEASE DO!" was my reply. "You don't have to explain anything. I want her in capable hands as fast as possible." I later learned that he did not have great confidence in the reassuring words that he spoke to me.

The pediatric trauma team was professional and gentle at the same time. They put on a cervical collar in case of spinal cord injury and began to approach her from all angles and perspectives. A social worker needed to get basic information from me, but when I expressed that at that particular moment I needed to be right next to my confused and terrified girl while she was being peppered with question after question, the social worker pushed me through to this position. After years of working hard to be attuned to the needs of my children, I spoke words of comfort in a calm voice. These words came almost automatically after lots and lots and lots of practice doing the same for both of our girls in their early days, months, and years with us. "Are you sure you are my mommy?" pierced my ears and heart. Even though my girl was confused and didn't know who I was, she did respond to my voice. I heard an observant team member say, "Mom is calming." They let me remain right by her side for the duration.

CT scans, x-rays, and ultrasounds were performed one right after another. As she moved through the scans, I sang special songs into her ear that were a part of her earliest days in our family. "Skidamarink-adink-adink, skidamarink-adoo, I love you" and a special song I made up just for her during her early difficult adjustment days in our home flowed out from my heart and voice. Each medical professional showed mercy on mother and child as they communicated that one test after another revealed no structural or internal damage. We heard the message over and over again that she was extremely lucky/fortunate/blessed. Both my young daughter and I came face to face with raw vulnerability, mortality, and the fact that life can change in an instant.

After several hours and many negative tests, Dad and sister arrived. Our precious girl was beginning to fully return to us. I told her that when her Daddy walked in the door, I would most likely cry. She understood. As soon as I saw Mark, it all came out.

In the quiet of the night in that ICU room, I often rose from my resting spot, put my hand on her beautiful face, and let the tears cascade from my eyes. Around 4 am, the cervical collar was removed, and we both relaxed into several hours of deep sleep. The next afternoon, our precious daughter got up and walked out of the hospital with her mom right by her side. Concussion was the diagnosis, and there was not a sore muscle in her body.

At some point, I realized that I needed to start putting words to the crashing waves of gratitude that filled my heart and mind during these days. I started making a list. It included the fact there were four adults on the scene when this accident happened. Each of us played a critical role in getting help and comforting the three young witnesses to this fall. I thanked God for our miracle and for mulch. The tree from which my daughter fell stands in a neglected corner of our back yard. Years of leaf fall and leaves blown into this corner created a nature pillow for our girl to land upon.

I was grateful for all of the personal work I had done in yoga and meditation. I had practiced remaining present and calm in the midst of difficulties. This was like a final exam. One nurse's encouraging, "I wish all moms could be as calm as you are" pointed to progress made and the payoff of hard work. My daughter had also practiced deep breathing and calming strategies in the midst of anxious times. She was able to access stillness at critical moments. The intentional work I did around shifting my parenting paradigm was a gift during the terrifying hours after the fall. The "you are safe and I am with you" emphasis was critical to impart to my petrified child who didn't even know who I was for a time. Our people cared for us well during difficult days.

I was even able to be grateful for lice. Forty-eight hours after the fall, it became obvious that lice were on my children's heads. I am a former OCD, over the edge, lice responder. Having lice was quickly put into proper perspective. After uttering a few cuss words and a big, "really?!", we arranged for a mobile lice buster to come to our home. I felt like a regular mom dealing with regular kid stuff. That was a gift.

The list could go on and on.

For weeks and months and as each anniversary rolls around after this fall, I experience an emotional roller coaster - anxious to weepy to filled with gratitude. When we birth or adopt children into our hearts and lives, we become extremely vulnerable. I have heard someone say that being a parent is like walking around in life with our heart exposed on our sleeve.

Most of us don't spend much time thinking about that because it is much too vulnerable and frightening. For any of us who truly love, our hearts can be crushed and devastated in an instant.

A week after her tumble to the ground, our girl was cleared to ease back into life and school as she recovered. On the day that I first took her back to school for an hour's stay, I felt like I was dropping a newborn off at daycare on her first day of life. My plan was to take a walk and be within ten minutes in case she needed to leave early. In the middle of the walk, I needed to find a restroom. After striking out at several places, I headed to my church. While I was there, I checked my email and received these words from my dear friend Jan. She put into words what I had been unable to clearly articulate:

"I feel the fear of all the 'what ifs' that come with such an accident. My prayers are with you as you move through all these and many more emotions surrounding this event. Thanks be to God for the power of grace that touched your daughter in that fall. For me, I don't understand grace, but I believe you were touched by it, and it continues to surround her."

I tell this story with great tenderness and awe for parents who have walked a similar road but experienced a very different outcome. Deep in my heart dwells empathy for the brutal possibility of losing a child, and yet I don't fully know it. This experience only magnifies and intensifies the questions around the mystery of miracles within my soul. I hold onto the belief that even if we had a different outcome on that day, grace would still be a part of our story. But it would have been a much more severe grace.

In the midst of our daughter's four names is the word "Grace." The Chinese name that she was given by her early caretakers can be interpreted "sunshiny blessing from heaven." In days, months, and years ahead, I will continue to ponder and wrestle with this very literal grace and blessing in my life.

As the one-year anniversary of the tree fall approached and the memories of a day blanketed with mercy and grace rose up to surface level, my heart raced accompanied by a stomach that flipped and flopped. The story could have ended in tragedy, yet we were all spared. The "why God does it happen this way sometimes, and sometimes not" questions persist. The "what ifs" still occasionally flow through my mind and haunt me. These moments are always followed by a desire to fall face down, spread eagle on the floor with gratitude for the grace sprinkled all around our family on that particular evening.

Just after the tree fall anniversary, our neighbor and his dad were up on the roof. There was a fall. Our local first responders were on the scene within minutes, just like on the day that our girl tumbled down. A memory rose up for one of the emergency workers. He recalled being on this street and the brick home two houses down. In the midst of tending to another fallen family member, he sought out our neighbor

Yasmin, mom of three young children. He hesitantly and in a hushed tone asked a question. "Ma'am, there was a little girl who fell from a tree. Over there. Two houses down. It was a really big fall. Do you know if she is ok? In this job, we never get to find out how the story ends. Is she normal?"

When our girl fell, we had only lived in our new home for two months. Yasmin did not know us by name on that day and did not even know which of our daughters had fallen. She now knows our names but when questioned by the fireman, she wasn't sure who fell. "Well, one of the girls plays soccer and darts around speedily wherever she goes and the other is our babysitter. So, yes, she is normal." Follow up questions and answers reassured this skeptical guy that in fact on that day, the story had a happy ending. The alternative endings are too painful for this mother's heart to dwell upon. It is a relief when the "what ifs" that ricochet within my mind are quieted.

As this anniversary came and went, I shared my deepest thoughts and feelings with my spiritual formation group. In response, a gentle and quiet lady who I barely know told of a visual often shared by her minister. He speaks of a ladder that he calls "the thin space between heaven and earth." This space was where we resided on that 2014 autumn day. God reached down as we begged and pleaded upward. No matter the outcome on that day, I cling to the idea that this thin space exists for all, come joy or sorrow.

Our family took in deeply and was touched by the care and concern of the emergency worker who does his job day in and day out without the gratification, or devastation, of knowing where it all leads. Our girl decided to write a letter that we did our best to get in front of those specific individuals who cared for us so well on our miracle day. This letter goes out to all who work, serve, heal, and participate in miracles without intimate and detailed knowledge of the grace that they impart moment by moment. In reality, that is each one of us.

Dear EMS workers,

Hello. I am the 11-year old girl who fell from the tree, in her backyard October 17 2014. I am writing this letter to you because one of my neighbors had to call you guys and while someone was there, they asked about me. I am now 12 years old and am doing great. Of course I am hitting puberty, so I have my emotional troubles, but it was only a concussion that I have suffered. I am in the 7th grade and am doing Common Core 1 (9th grade math) and my grades are just where I like them. I want to assure you that I am doing great. Thank you for saving my life (maybe) and for asking about me. I know it can be hard not knowing how the people you save are doing due to all the patient confidentiality and stuff. Thank you again for wondering and I am glad that I am able to at least fill you in. Have a wonderful Thanksgiving.

Sincerely,

The girl who fell from the magnolia

In the gospel of Luke, I read, "Mary treasured up all these things and pondered them in her heart" (Luke 2:19, New International Version). That is how I approach this miracle within my family. The mystery of the miracle is an ongoing wrestling match within, and our particular story only magnifies the questions. I have no answers. I am learning to be content in the mystery.

Though my daughter has healed and life has moved forward, this is still a very tender story held within my mother's heart. There is a scar of reminder that sometimes rubs against my soul and the reality of the utter vulnerability of being this thing called mom. Many prefer to deny and repress this common to every parent possibility of having our hearts crushed in a matter of seconds. Letting this fragile reality come to the surface on occasion offers up a more profound gratitude and joy around each moment with this child which in turn extends to each person that I love. Knowing more fully the fragility of life invites me to deeper love and greater joy. It is a gateway to living with an open and vulnerable heart not only for those I love most but also to those I once deemed as "other."

Reflection

One of my favorite Isaiah verses begins, "I will give you the treasures of darkness, riches stored in secret places" (Isaiah 45:3, NRSV). When I look back over some of the darkest and most challenging times in life, I did in fact receive treasures and riches during those days. It certainly did not feel that way in the midst of living the moments, but with time and reflection, it is the reality.

Life has taught me the truth of Brené Brown's words, "There is a full spectrum of human emotions, and when we numb the dark we numb the light."[24] In order to experience the grace and joy all around me, I have to open myself to pain and suffering. When I work hard to push away the more difficult human feelings, I am also denying myself access to the beauty of life.

So rather than desire safety, security, and smooth sailing for my children, I borrow a phrase from one of my favorite authors, Anne Lamott. I wish for "traveling mercies" as they encounter the wide scope of human experience. In fact, "traveling mercies" has become the heartbeat of many of my prayers and requests on behalf of those I love.

CHAPTER 8

GRACE AND "THE OTHER"

You have to be able to imagine lives that are not yours.
Wendell Berry

hen I bought into the idea that my particular religious herd was fundamentally different from the rest of our fellow humans, the result was that walls were erected between me and anyone labeled as "other." Not only did I have a judge and jury in my mind ready to condemn myself, they were also making judgments about all those around me. This mindset led to suspicion and an inability to fully enjoy and connect with others. I was too busy sizing them up to determine if they were in or out. In time and as I entered into relationship with various people, I began to see the walls that the herd had built around me.

I am borrowing a term that my pastor Lisa coined – otherizing. In the denomination of my youth and to this day across many conservative places of worship, anyone who is deemed "other" is often cast aside, labeled as a sinner, feared, and/or put into boxes that encourage detachment rather than relationship. When we otherize, we reject the common bonds we have with all of humanity and cut ourselves off from people who can help us understand diverse points of view, live in authentic community, and practice loving our "neighbors." The result is that we fall prey to pride, arrogance, and the necessity to be right about our own perspectives.

Liberals can be just as guilty as conservatives. Any shade of dogmatism creates a world full of "others." But because the early messages imprinted within my heart and mind were of the more religiously fundamental and conservative nature, my initial challenge was to open up to those who were otherized by the tradition of my youth. Yet, interestingly, as my beliefs and ideas have shifted, I am now faced with the task of more fully loving those who represent my earlier religious training. Whenever and however I designate anyone in my life as "other," I must then take action to open my heart and mind to the other's point of view.

On the first go round of parenting, I mostly hung out with like-minded parents. I naively and mistakenly believed that this would offer a shield of protection around my children. Participating in international adoption cracked and then blew open the door to relationship with interesting people, many who come at life from very different perspectives.

My personal journey went something like this: I first began to listen to the voice of others, I was forced to listen to the voices of my children, and then I received the grace to listen to my own voice. At times, I worked so hard to protect the religious turf in my mind that I could not look up and out to truly see the beauty in those so often marked as other. In reality the questions and push back on the status quo of my earliest religion was there from the start. I just needed to cultivate and receive the freedom and courage to entertain other ideas and points of view.

As we interact with people in our daily lives, we rarely know the backstory of those who cross our paths. Public encounters with strangers or people we don't know well can be fraught with misunderstanding and judgments. The reality is that each person in any encounter comes to that moment with a story, a history. It may be full of pain and suffering. We just don't know.

I recently observed ignorance like this when my friend, who sometimes walks with a cane due to rheumatoid arthritis, was mocked at our local grocery store. A stranger yelled to her "Why are you using a cane? You are too young for that." It stung. She had been judged right there in the produce aisle. Reading her account of this on Facebook pierced my heart. I have also felt the sting of a stranger's judgment.

Going to the library with my daughters is one of my greatest joys. On a beautiful, sunny day, my elementary aged girls bounded from the car with excitement. The youngest had just left the car and called back to me, "Mom can you grab my bag?" That's how we lug the big stacks of books that we mine from the shelves. I picked up the bag and a stranger said, "NOOOOOOO, she needs to learn to do things for herself." There was a day when that would have stung and my defensive self would have responded either internally or out loud, "Do you have any idea how hard I have worked to get this child to trust and attach to me. What is the big flipping deal about getting that bag for her?" Thankfully on that day I said, "Is that your perspective? I disagree, this time…" We are always working on independence, but it is a careful dance. I was at peace with my choice to help on that day. Interactions like these are great reminders that most people don't know my family's backstory. And I often don't know the particular life experiences of those I cross paths with on a daily basis.

Danielle was a beautiful 3rd grade girl. Being a reading buddy group leader with six children in her class was a highlight of my week. Before the experience of raising children affected by trauma, I would have had some very strong thoughts and opinions on the fountain of tall tales that bubbled from this child's mouth. But my perspective had changed. She spun out fantasies involving her parents' professions, income level, and the many adventures of the family of her imagination. She seemed to believe that if she spoke her wishes out loud, they would come true. I had enough information to know that her dad was not involved in her life. As I encountered her outrageous stories, my thoughts became, "I wonder what kind of trauma is going on in her home?" I don't know the answer to that question, but I do know that mid-year Danielle told me one of the only reliable things she ever spoke to me. Her grandmother had come down from Chicago and soon the two of them were leaving together and heading north. Leaving her mom, who despite what pain and suffering had happened in this relationship, she loved and idolized. I imagined her settling in with Grandma in a cold and distant place. She offered words of hope: "I will be back by 4th grade." That was not how this story unfolded.

As I interact with strangers and those I barely know, the lesson is to offer grace and mercy to each one that crosses my path. I wonder what led that lady to yell hurtful words to my friend in the grocery store? She certainly wasn't mindful of the backstories of others. And what about the lady in front of the library? What life experience led her to interject herself into my family on that day? And how about precious Danielle? I bet my heart would break over the details of her backstory. We just never know.

During the years that I worked so hard to transform my parenting paradigm, Becky Bailey's *Conscious Discipline* introduced me to so many new and useful ideas. Among them was the idea of "positive intent." Loosely paraphrased, this means assuming the best intentions of others. Theoretically, this makes sense to many of us, but in practical everyday living and parenting, it can be downright difficult to practice. Rather than approaching our children or anyone else we interact with as "pushing my button," "just trying to irritate me," or "out to get me," we can choose to see it differently. As Bailey points out, we really don't have a clue what is going on inside of someone else and what motivates them to behave as they do. Since we can only guess at the motivations and thoughts of others, we might as well make them up in a positive light.[25] In other words, presume that others are acting with positive intent toward themselves, given their very own circumstances and story. It isn't always about me...

I love to shop at Target, but there is one checkout person that always gets under my skin. She and her sour look are almost always there when I enter the store. I wonder what has or is going on in the life of someone who presents such grouchiness toward customers? Once when she was rude to me, we got into an exchange of words. This was complicated by the fact that my then five year old was observing everything that I said and did. Yes, I felt somewhat justified and better in the moment when I let some words fly, but it did not last. My heart sank as I then had to try and justify my actions to my daughter. My conscience won out, and I ended up owning my own role in a heated exchange and then returning to apologize for my part in the fray.

Positive intent is approaching others with the conviction and belief that they are just trying to take care of themselves in the best way they know. Sometimes with children, that can look like a raging fit or an icy silence. The ultimate goal is to teach and model healthy ways to express emotions, but that takes a lot of repetition, time, self awareness, and energy. We will be more successful with that when we approach our children or anyone else in life with the underlying belief of positive intent. Bailey says it like this, "The truth is that we make up motivations. How we choose to make them up effects (sic) both the person we attribute the motives to and ourselves. If you make up negative motives you will be guarded, ready for defense, or attack. If you make up positive motives, you will be relaxed and calm."[26]

This is definitely easier said than done, but after putting this idea into practice every now and then, I see the truth and wisdom in it. A few years later, I experienced the power of positive intent in the very same Target with the very same clerk. I brought three reusable bags up to the register. She chose the smallest of the bags and with great determination and effort, stuffed all of the items into this one bag. It was overflowing. I offered another bag at one point, and she actively shook her head and with seeming delight said, "no." She was going to get them all into the one bag. On some days, this would have irritated me. On that day, I was in a relatively Zen kind of place and told myself a list of possible explanations for her actions: maybe she likes a bagging challenge; she is saving Target a nickel or two; maybe she gets a bonus for this kind of thing; I wonder if this is what keeps her job interesting for her. I was making it all up for sure, but in the light of positive intent. It was a much nicer walk out to my car on that day. I walked away in a state of calm and peace rather than frustration and embarrassment. And I didn't have to explain to my children any questionable behavior or go back in and apologize for anything that time.

When I can pull it off, positive intent is my friend. I don't need to waste precious time or energy writing negative scripts for others and attributing motivation to their every move. The bottom line is that I am not a mind reader. A posture of curiosity and positive intent, even if it is only inside of my thoughts, leads to greater compassion and grace for each and every "other" that I interact with along my way.

Many of us have either been told or directly experienced the "it's who you know" phenomenon in social, educational, or work life. Despite the inequity of such a principle, it is alive and well and inescapable within our culture. I have also come to realize that the "it's who you know" concept also applies to our biases, prejudices, and fears toward those we deem as "other." During the time when I raised my sons, I taught them to be kind to all. But I rarely sought out the company of people who were so often labeled "other" by my religion or culture. As an adoptive mom, there were more natural opportunities to interact with people of varying races, religions, and perspectives. I accepted the invitation to interact with and get to know a diverse group of people.

A particular overnight field trip comes to mind. The excitement had been palpable in our home for well over a week. Our girl, who goes through life with most of her emotions on the inside, had been visibly joyous with anticipation for this rite of passage, an end of elementary days journey to Washington DC. Her dad and I took delight in the expressions of pleasure and anticipation as the day of departure approached. We all held our breath as the never ending North Carolina winter dumped freezing rain and cancelled school a mere twenty-four hours ahead of take off time. Our daughter took great care as she placed each carefully chosen item into a small suitcase and backpack.

After a 5 am wake up, a little breakfast, and a last bit of shared contagious excitement, we headed to the school. After unloading our luggage, we claimed our spots on the big bus. Knowing that we were facing several hours of sitting, I got out and walked around. I headed to the restroom and was warmly greeted with a beautiful smile and a hug. Melissa – pronounced Ma-lee-sa – was one of the children in my book buddy group a few years back. We had a special bond. Over time and as we read books together each week, she shared some intimate details of her family's life and story as Mexican immigrants. On the morning of the field trip, as we chatted about the exciting days ahead, she said, "My dad is crying. It is hard for him to say goodbye." I hugged her and then walked back toward the bus. As she connected with her dad one last time, I looked deep into his eyes and said, "We will take good care of your daughter." What was the story behind those teary eyes? What had he seen and lived to have such emotion around this three day parting?

As an adoptive mom, I crossed paths with various family configurations including those with two moms. Such a union was much maligned in the denomination of my youth. We first met along the regular and mundane road of childhood activities. It began with speaking hello as we dropped off and picked up our children. It went a little deeper as we chatted and shared as mothers, of children born of our hearts but not our bodies. At first, such a lifestyle was uncomfortable to me as the years of hell and damnation proclamations rattled through my brain. But way down in my deepest heart I always suspected that God saw it differently and thus could I.

Recently as I sat watching my girl play soccer, one of these moms came up from behind and tapped me on the shoulder. Her lovely smile greeted me with warmth and acceptance. I am so glad she could not see into my conflicted soul during our early meeting days, or maybe she could and offered me extreme grace. Looking back, irrational fear and the messages of my youth put up a wall, but thankfully barriers can be broken. I have observed how this family is beautiful and full of love. My friend is a good and kind mother and wife.

Her daughter was trying a new sport and mine was in the goal for the first time in a very long time. We had five minutes of connection as we talked of birthdays and the death of her mother. We experienced honest human connection. There was nothing at all to fear. What is it that has quelled the damning voices inside my mind? It is the face-to-face, friend-to- friend interactions with "others" that has led the way. They are in fact not "others" at all.

Which of us has not changed our hearts and minds about a particular prejudice toward a "type" of person after truly getting to know them, one individual at a time? When I keep "the other" at arm's length, then I am comfortable fearing or disparaging entire groups of people, even if it is just within my mind. When I label another as poor, homeless, Muslim, gay, transgender, liberal, conservative, or any other adjective, then I give up the option to truly listen to and interact with someone as my fellow human. It is in the midst of everyday interactions and conversations that my heart and mind open up to change.

Within family, when someone we love reveals being part of a previously feared or disdained group, we almost always move forward together given time, communication, understanding, and true love. It is rare to truly renounce someone we love over such matters. When rejection of a loved one is the choice, there is always great pain, suffering, and destruction within the one scorned as well as the larger family or community. Kent Annan, author on the topic of faith and justice, says it this way: "It's vital for us to enter into the truth of other people's lives. We'll see the world differently."[27] I have found this to be true.

One day as my older daughter was about to leave elementary school, I needed to quickly buy a gift for her to take to a birthday party. I stopped by an intimate, fun, eclectic shop full of interesting items. As I browsed, it became clear that the store clerk wanted to engage in conversation. Despite my hurried pace, I decided to slow down and interact with this fellow human traveler.

Suddenly, she poured out her heart. She had just experienced a broken romantic relationship with her girlfriend. Her pain was compounded by the choice to keep this part of her life secret from her mom and dad. She expressed her fear of rejection and damnation by the childhood religious folks so interwoven in her family's story. She told me that she was working on a letter, a desperate plea for acceptance and love. She had tentative hope that maybe, just maybe, minds and hearts and souls would soften toward her.

Neither of us quite knew how we got to this vulnerable space, but my own heart whispered to treat this with tenderness and care. A response welled up from deep within me. She and I shared the kinship of two hearts that want to be known and loved. I spoke up. "Most mothers, given time and space, will come to accept and love unconditionally their child."

Parenting matters in so many different ways. We teach and model values, character, and how to truly love one another. At their core, each of my children is a unique soul. If their deepest, truest selves include a characteristic or belief that makes me uncomfortable or goes against a conviction that I hold dear, I am then faced with a critical choice. I can expend energy trying to suppress or deny the reality within one that I love, or I can walk alongside and do my best to have empathy and compassion and make peace within and without. I, as a mom, possess a great deal of power to either add or subtract pain and suffering to the journeys of my children. If I choose to "otherize" my own child, I have then decided to cause them pain and suffering. I choose a different path. I commit to loving each of my children well, no matter what comes.

I was playing cards with one of my sons and shared my story of the store clerk encounter. His response was, "Mothers should rule the world." In many ways, we do. If we wear garments of grace, then a compassionate and kind kingdom will come.

So if there is a people group that makes me squirm or I just don't understand, the challenge is to live a life that will cross paths with such individuals. Sometimes they show up in random daily interactions. Other times they move in next door or are present in my own family. If I open my ears and heart to form relationship, there is always much to learn. It truly is so very often who I know.

Reflection

Dear Formerly "Other,"

I am sorry. I am willing to soften my heart, put aside judgment, and see you as fully human, just like me. I am ready to listen to your voice and your story. I want to do the hard work of reconciliation. If you will join me, the indescribable gifts of grace and love are available to each of us. Please forgive my misdeeds and errant thoughts toward you.

With love and grace,
Tricia

CHAPTER 9

LETTING GO

*Love in action is a harsh and dreadful thing
compared with love in dreams.*
Fyodor Dostoyevsky in *The Brothers Karamazov*

Though most parents assent to the belief that the goal of parenting is to raise children who ultimately become independent adults, the actual and sometimes brutal emotional realities required from the parental side of this equation can be formidable. Letting go begins in the earliest days, just after we are bestowed the title of mom or dad. The opportunities ramp up as our children reach adolescence, adulthood, and beyond. I, as a mom, can put up a fight against this necessary surrender, or I can work to make peace with a process that often feels so very unnatural. This choice is ever before me.

Raising children has offered me the sometime unwelcome invitation to let go. In the early days, each of my kids was utterly dependent upon me for their every need. I was encouraged to form healthy attachment and in a sense, become one with them. But just around the corner, the separation process began. At first, their dad and I let the safety tether out the slightest bit, with the ability to pull it back in if necessary. Before long, there were daily opportunities for greater release - from clothing to friends to how to spend time and out into ever widening circles of choice. Sometimes this process felt natural and at other times it was heart wrenching.

I quickly learned that the whether or not to wear a jacket discussion is small potatoes compared to some of the stuff coming down the road. My children are gifts and individual souls that do not belong to me. I am entrusted with their care and teaching for a season, but it is healthy and right for them to head toward a life of making their own choices and decisions. This eventually included what to consume, lifestyle decisions, faith expression, political views, relationships, and the list goes on and on and on. They dream dreams and pursue paths. Some align with my wishes as a mom, and some don't.

One critical distinction that I had to learn as a parent is that my children are not an extension of me. Each one of them will make their own mistakes, forge their own pathways, and discover joy in their own places. It is my job to be a coach, teacher, and encourager along the way, but I must untangle my own ego and expectations from their journey. We are separate individuals.

It is painful to watch my children struggle, suffer, or seemingly veer off course. During such times, my desire is to respond in love and with genuine heart and head attunement.

Yet I am so easily gripped with fear. Throughout motherhood, this fear has shown up in the form of a low rumbling anxiety as well as wake up in the night, paralyzing terror. Neither one proved helpful.

I wasted a tremendous amount of parental energy during times when I desperately attempted to fix and control my kids. The mental gymnastics I used to perform seeking to affect, influence, or control my children or their choices were exhausting. Sometimes when things were rocky, I looked for someone to blame – myself, my husband, a friend, or a teacher. I often talk the talk of trust and release of my children into God's hands, but I sometimes stumble in the execution of this belief.

At this stage of my motherhood journey, my desire is to live in a more contemplative space on the matter of my children and their lives. Rather than list out Tricia's agenda for each of them, I often symbolically hold them in my hands, lift them up to God, and release them to God's grace and care. Sometimes it is a severe relinquishment.

There are certain times when it is wise for me to speak up and offer gentle guidance. That most often depends upon the age of my child and sometimes whether or not they ask for my thoughts. I have learned that it is often wise to say, "Do you want some ideas? Do you want to know what I think?" It takes restraint because my impulse is often to spout off advice and offer all sorts of solutions to a problem. There are times that it seems wisest to be silent, even if my heart breaks as I hold my thoughts and tongue. Navigating these nuances and responses requires mindful discernment.

To master the art of letting go at an appropriate pace and time, with a heart full of love and hope, is my worthy intention. As I release my children, I desire to dwell in the mystery and faithfulness of God and to find joy and delight as they discover and live out their own dreams and lives. My children have great treasures to share with me, but if I can't see beyond my own expectations and desires for them, I am going to miss out. As they grow up and out into their own places, I get to practice living out my beliefs. A valuable first step is to loosen my grip and gently let go.

A few years ago, our family moved out of the home we had lived in for twenty-three years. The physical and emotional tasks around this move forced a lesson in letting go. I often found myself asking this question: What can fall aside and what shall remain?

On the October 1991 day that we moved into our beautiful two story 1960's brick home, I snuck away from the moving day chaos and headed to a local lab. "Yes," the lab worker said, "you are pregnant." It was a joyful day on so many levels as I learned that our third child was on the way. This son spent his entire growing up days in this house.

As I prepared for our move, sorting through keepsakes and memorabilia with each of our three sons was bittersweet. What was of value to them at the end of high school and college had shifted. It was poignant to walk alongside as each son decided what he wanted to take forward and what could fall aside. Their own memories and choices often trumped my opinions on the matter. Only on rare occasions did I say, "I think you might want to have that one day" and slip it into a keepsake box.

Their particular choices didn't always align with mine. Some of the things they chose to carry forward did not include me in the story. Each one had drama roles, team participation, or reminiscences with friends that were special to them but happened without mom by their side. They are three individual young men who have chosen their own paths. That was the goal, yet the deep realization of this place in time can sometimes bring me to tears.

When I was twenty-nine years old and expecting our third child, life seemed as if it would go on almost forever. Yet, it passed so quickly. Sometimes I feel nostalgic and long for earlier days, yet at the same time I feel excited and hopeful about the possibilities of living life in a new space. Realizing that I almost for sure have less days left on this earth than I have already lived helps bring focus to life. Well beyond the material choices of what to take and what to leave behind are the bigger issues of how I want to live life. What do I take along from the past and what do I leave behind? How will I spend my hours, days, and years? What remains?

This beloved verse reverberates throughout my being as I ponder this important question. "And now these three remain: faith, hope and love. But the greatest of these is love" (I Corinthians 13:13, New International Version). As I rapidly move toward the day when my children and I no longer share an address, there are endless prospects and an excitement around the choices before me. With gratitude for the past and the path traveled, I also look forward to the shifts and transformation ahead. The possibilities beckon. One thing I do know is this. The steps ahead must always be grounded in faith, hope, and the greatest of these, love.

When I was a baby, a family friend gifted to me a Christmas stocking made of felt. It spells out PATRICIA at the top and is adorned with Santa and other Christmasy symbols. This creation inspired a tradition, and my mom made a similar one for each member of our growing family, including her grandchildren.

Each year, I hang my stocking with hope and care, and Santa always delivers. I don't remember the exact exchange, but at some point before my first Christmas as a wife, my mom delivered the PATRICIA stocking to me to hang in our newlywed home. So for my first married Christmas, I hung it up. I am so glad Santa followed and found me in my new family.

On December 21, 2014, our youngest son asked his beautiful girlfriend to marry him. We already loved this young lady deeply and were so very excited to add one more daughter to the crazy Wilson mix. The promise of plus one to our family was shared, discussed, and celebrated throughout the Christmas season.

For ten years, seven stockings hung from our mantle. In 2014 as the year's festivities were on the downhill slide, I looked up above our fireplace, and my heart and stomach lurched. I counted and recounted. One, two, three, four, five, six. Only six stockings hung from the mantle. After closer examination, the AWOL stocking belonged to our newly engaged son. In a wounded mom tone of voice, I said with disbelief, "You took your stocking?!" His reply was approximately, "Yeah." In that moment, I didn't clarify his motive, meaning, or message behind this event, but in following days, I tossed it over and over in my heart and brain.

It is symbolic. Yes, this youngest son and his bride will always and forever be a part of our family. But at the same time, we are all transitioning to a different center. His would soon be the family that he and his fiancé commit to, beginning during their engagement and sealed with an "I do." The rest of us would soon be more appropriately referred to as extended family.

And though my primary emotion was joy, it was mixed with nostalgia and periodic sadness. To where did those years since I held him in my arms and rocked him to sleep disappear? What happened to the little blond haired, sparkly blue-eyed boy that would go outside for hours and hit a golf ball, bounce a basketball, or kick a football? This parenthood train is one that at times I wish I could slow down, but it just rumbles down the track.

Taking down Christmas decorations and returning to life's routines is for me always a melancholy event. On this year, I delayed it as long as practically possible. It marked the last Christmas that our five children were centered in their nuclear family. Intentionally savoring the special moments all during the holidays intensified the awareness that things were getting ready to shift. I wondered where, or even if, he would hang his stocking in the years ahead...

Weeks later, I asked, "Why did you take your stocking to your house?" His response was, "I needed something to carry my stuff in. I used it like a bag." I am still not sure whether that is the entire truth, but this situation did beckon me to ponder and consider one concrete aspect of letting go as a mother.

Ultimately, my son returned this stocking to me and allows me to hang it on the mantle each year. Right next to his, another bearing the name of his wife has been added to the mix. If they are able to travel to our home at Christmas time, Santa fills both of them. He requested that his grandmother create two new and different felt stockings that hang on the mantle of his faraway home each Christmas. Rather than an exercise in subtraction, there is always room for another, both on the mantle and in our hearts.

Over a span of nine months, two of our sons got married. Along with the celebration and excitement, this was also a time for me to be mindful and consider what kind of mother-in-law I want to be. For about half of my mothering life, I was mom to only boys. Three sons made for a lively and boisterous life. I vaguely remember the first time I heard the following ditty: a son is a son until he takes a wife; a daughter is a daughter all of her life. I did not much like the sentiment, but I realized that within American culture, it sometimes feels this way. As we approached the first wedding, I wrote these words as a message to all who may enter our family:

Dear future daughter-in-law,

I have been blessed with a gracious and non-interfering mother-in-law. Though I know she has deep convictions and opinions, she has only given advice when asked. I am grateful that she is a person whose perspective I respect and is approachable when I want to hear from her. My goal and desire is to pass on to you this gift that she gave to me.

From the moment his conception was made known to me, I dedicated this son to God. It has been a delight and joy to watch him grow up and become a man. Part of that process has at times been painful, but it is deeply satisfying to see him becoming the man that he was meant to be. It gives me great pleasure to know that he has chosen to partner with you in this journey of life.

Though for many years I was the most important woman in his life, it is most appropriate and healthy that you now occupy that space. There is a power shift that has been in motion since the day that you entered his life. It brings me great joy to see the love that you have for one another.

During this season, I have paid particular attention to those around me who have walked this road before me. I see and hear stories of mothers of sons who struggle to let go and of those who travel this road beautifully. My intention is to emulate the latter. When I stray from this intent, I invite you to gently remind me of this letter and commitment to you.

I hope that we can enjoy common interests together and in the context of our larger family. It is my desire to be one among your many encouragers and friends. I wish for you and your husband to laugh each day, to enjoy life separately and together as you grow up alongside each other. It is not smooth sailing that I dream of for you, but a hope that through the joys and sorrows of life you will experience traveling mercies and the gentle hand of God.

As your soon to be sister-in-law learned several years back as she wrestled with sharing her brothers' love with other females, love

*does not have to be divided as a family grows, but it can multiply.
We already love you and look forward to the multiplication of
love as we share life together as family.*

With deep gratitude and love,

Your future mother-in-law

Many plans and hopes and dreams had been imagined
and focused toward this March weekend. Our middle son was
to be wed to his beautiful, full of life fiancée. Much care and
planning and negotiation preceded the four-day celebration.
The weather forecast was for rain and a dip in the spring
temperatures. Many people from many places descended upon
St. Louis to stand alongside and be with our boy and his bride.
There were lots of moving parts, people doing their share, and
now it was go time.

As parents of the groom, our big event and
responsibility was around the rehearsal dinner. It was time to
set up for the evening. I got into our rental car, put it into
reverse, and smiled at my youngest son and his wife in the
backseat. I looked into my side mirror and saw a big dumpster,
but I missed the large steel hooks protruding from its side.

After a screech and scrape of metal against metal, a
little advice from the man in the backseat, and a panic response
that led to the meeting of the left rear bumper and a brick wall,

I took a big, deep breath. "Now I have to tell your dad" came out of my mouth. Heart pounding and feeling a little sick and sheepish, I drove around to meet my most loving and gracious husband.

No one, most of all me, wanted this unfortunate car vs dumpster situation to cloud or color the event before us. After apologies, contrition, and an agreement that it was most important to put this aside until much later, we traveled to our downtown destination. I practiced deep breathing and resolved to settle down for this most important celebration before us. My backseat passenger and his dad noticed my elevated stress level and massaged my shoulders to assist in relief. It was a generous and welcome laying on of hands.

After an hour of technology set up, a space in which I can feel most inept, we worked through the issues and were on our way to rehearse for the wedding ceremony. From that point, all went well on this day. The energy was high, relationships were formed and renewed, and stories were shared. We enjoyed the video of bride and groom childhood photos set to sentimental songs. The video that I lovingly prepared then transitioned into a visual narrative of this couple's story. I went to bed most grateful.

Around 6:00 am, we heard groaning and crying in the loft above our room. Our youngest girl complained of stomach pains and restless sleep. After some discussion, the diagnosis was that it was most likely a case of eating a bit "off diet" the previous night coupled with nervous energy around her groomsmaid (she was going to stand on her brother's side) role for the day. I headed off to an early morning pre-wedding yoga class, a mutual passion and pursuit with the bride, and soaked up the relaxing and centering instruction. For me, this was a most desirable start to a wedding day. The forecasted rain and cold had given way to blue skies.

As I rolled back to our home base, news of our littlest girl getting sick in the bathroom and her return to sleep greeted me. I still held out hope that this was a one and done situation. After all, this was a very big day. Her brother was getting married. Dresses, shoes, hairstyles, and ceremony had been talked of for months. This was no day for a stomach bug.

We were on a fairly unforgiving schedule, continued to march through the day, and showed up at the places required. We arrived at the bride's home with dresses in tow. We brought makeup and hair supplies and were ready to roll. Having a sister-in-law afforded our girls a much more stylish look than mom could provide. Sister-in-law got to curling and twisting and making beautiful. But the stomach continued to ache.

I felt a great deal of tension and turmoil as we navigated the next hours. Between getting my own clothes and makeup in place, I checked in with our daughter. Any change? Do you think you are going to be sick, or the more hopeful do you feel any better now? The look on her face was not a promising one. I tried to isolate her in case we were dealing with a virus while also knowing that if that was in fact the verdict, she had been around all these people for the past twenty-four hours. I hoped with all my might that she would be able to be a part of her brother's most important day. My husband and I huddled to make contingency plans. We clarified that mother and father of the groom being present as much as possible was the primary goal for this day.

Pictures were taken, and she was able to be a part. We traveled to the church. She and I located restrooms, talked, wandered, and agonized. I tried to comfort and be steady and realistic. It was emotionally draining. It would be devastating for her to miss the wedding or the reception, or both. Our family really likes to eat and dance and celebrate together...

And then, I had clarity. We made one last dash to the bathroom. This was definitely a stomach bug. Once I leaned into what was and quit straining for what I wished to be, calm came over me, the mother of the groom. Our dear and gracious sister and brother-in-law took her to their hotel room. She was in good hands. I was relieved. As much as I wanted her there, now I could be fully present for our son. And the wedding began.

It was beautiful and poignant and my heart swelled with love for this boy who was entrusted to our care for such a short time. He heard words of wisdom, spoke powerful vows, and made and received promises as this new family was formed. It was holy ground and a celebration. My mother's heart was delighted and full.

Our peaked girl walked into the reception for a few moments but knew she needed to be elsewhere to give honor to her own body and situation. We all felt sad that she wasn't among us as we ate and laughed and danced. She had made fast friends on Friday with a 6th grade boy from New York City while kicking a soccer ball and playing video games. His mom reported that he had a thing for sassy girls and was so sad to hear of her situation. Our girl's sass had bowed down to sick on this particular day. He kept voicing hope that maybe she would come to the party for just a little while. I think he had hopes of dancing with our sassy girl.

During other segments of my journey, such an inopportune time for a fender bender and a stomach bug would have thrown me off balance in a more profound way. Though there were both deep disappointments and a wish for a partially different script on these days, the weekend was full of joy and laughter and tears and gratitude. We welcomed another beautiful daughter-in-law, and one more of our children had made a home with the one he loves most deeply.

On Sunday morning, our girl woke up after about 14 hours of sleep and was almost as good as new. There were fifteen awful hours that came at a most unfortunate time. As we looked out the window on this day, we witnessed another short-lived, snowy surprise. Sometimes the undesired or unpredictable happen. A benefit of letting go of that which we cannot control is a more peace-filled walk through life.

Despite the twists and unexpected detours along this weekend, we still experienced great joy and true family, permeated with hope and the beauty of new beginnings. I believe this is an accurate picture of life, particularly life in partnership with another. There will be times of exhilaration and contentment coupled with periods of pain and unexpected sorrow.

As I reflected on the many aspects of this wedding weekend, I was instructed and inspired. To each of my children as they partner up and form families, I offer this blessing: When things go a little bit or a great deal awry and the unexpected shows up in your days and years ahead, I wish you grace in each moment. I hope that you know true love and joy all along the way. I echo the words that were sung as I experienced an emotional mother-son dance and claim that sharing a name is a privilege and great joy. I am most honored to be family with you.

As the day approached for our middle son to exchange marriage vows with his fiancée, I received an email request from Sybil, the mother of the bride. She had a special wish. Her desire was for us to assemble a basket together. She wanted to fill it with favorite items representing each of our individual families as well as some that symbolized our children's new life together. From my perspective, it seemed like a kind gesture, but I could tell that this had deeper meaning to my new friend who would soon give her daughter in marriage. As the day approached, she made it clear that putting together this basket was her highest priority on the day before our children's union.

As I discussed this request with someone close to me, her wisdom shed light on the situation. This basket was a transition object. It symbolized the passing of our beloved children into their own nuclear family as well as sharing them within each of our larger families-what a beautiful invitation.

With small children who sometimes struggle to separate from mom and dad at night or when left in the care of others, a blankie or well-loved stuffed animal often serve as a transition object. When our daughter was distressed with the adjustment to the kindergarten separation, we each wore a special necklace or kept a carefully chosen rock in our pockets to symbolize connection even in the midst of separation. Marrying off a child requires a whole different level of remaining connected while at the same time accepting and making peace with healthy separation.

For my son's soon to be mother-in-law, there was magnified symbolism around the choosing and assembling of this basket. At this point in time, Sybil had struggled with illness for many years. The treatment options were diminishing. At the time of her daughter's wedding, she knew deep in her heart that her days upon this earth were numbered. I can only begin to imagine the depth and breadth of the emotions she experienced during the wedding weekend of her beloved daughter. Great joy was tinged with sorrow, grief, and celebration, all co-mingled within a mother's heart.

Sybil invited my daughters to help assemble this basket. One chose to do so and the other decided to run around outside and play soccer with her fast friend from New York. Together, we placed a book of poetry, a bottle of champagne, candles, and other carefully selected items into the basket. My daughter arranged the items and used her artistic skills to make it attractive. The next day, Sybil looked radiant and beautiful as we celebrated the marriage of our children.

Eight months later, my husband and I traveled back to St. Louis and entered the same church where our son was married. This time we celebrated and mourned Sybil's life and death. Many people showed up to grieve and remember and tell stories about this special lady. Her husband and children publicly spoke of the love, legacy, and gifts she imparted to so many during her life.

Though we rarely let it come into our highest consciousness, life on this earth together with those we love most will come to an end. The hope of heaven offers solace as we allow our hearts and minds to entertain such a parting. As mother, the releases are everyday and all along the way tasks. These add up and crescendo toward grander calls to truly let go. For me, the knowledge of an eventual ending of life together as we know it offers up the possibility and the grace to experience the full range of each and every moment as it appears. The ultimate gift is a beautiful yet sometimes severe grace that I have received in this journey as mom.

The journey of motherhood as well as life itself is one of letting go. No stage or season with our children is permanent but always flowing onward. Though there is grief around this, we are also extended the possibility of deeply knowing joy, beauty, grace, and true love. The poet Rainer Maria Rilke penned these words: "Is not impermanence the very fragrance of our days?" I answer a resounding yes to this inquiry. Thank you to each of my children for serving as teacher to your student mom. You are the most powerful instruments of grace in my most beautiful life.

ENDING

I wish that the ministers and people I consulted early in my questioning and doubting faith journey had been more at home with nuance. All questions don't need a definitive answer. I wish I had more fully passed along this perspective to our sons as they grew up. At this point in my journey, rather than being focused on dogma and doctrine, I am most certain that God's work and ways are indeed full of mystery. Living into this belief offers a great deal of grace for myself and others. I have come to agree with Richard Rohr who says, "We belong to a mystery far greater than our little selves and our little time."

Not so terribly long ago, I felt that I was personally falling apart along with my family. Recently, I was standing and pondering in a space that often invites reflection - our kitchen. As I chopped vegetables, the internal challenge was to identify two critical actions that had most shifted our family dynamic. Among a longer list are changes such as a healthy dietary commitment, exercise, yoga, meditation, reading books, and various therapies. These decisions were part of a larger puzzle - how to authentically move myself from a legalistic, fearful faith practice to a perspective saturated with grace. It was only after a complete breakdown of the promises made in my religious tradition that I was willing to put aside fear, seek new ways, and adopt grace above all. But for me, there are two specific changes that top the list of "Wilson family life-giving decisions."

The first is my own personal acknowledgement of the need for mental health support and then the pursuit of that. Several therapists have played a priceless role in guiding me to become my very best and true self. Pursuing this avenue was not encouraged in my background nor valued by many of the people who influenced my younger life. But it has certainly made a tremendous difference. When I am healthy, those I am in relationship are also healthier.

The second thing that came to mind is the decision for my husband to slowly step away from the high demands of his career and more fully partner at home and integrate into the family demands. Our earlier bargains and beliefs were not sufficient for the task of raising and supporting five children, two who began their lives in difficult places. I am so very grateful that in the midst of crisis we were able to begin taking baby steps toward a healthier way of being family. We are still very much along that pathway.

None of these shifts in my faith or family happened overnight. They have required years of negotiation and work and change. True shifting of mind and heart and action take a great deal of mindful attention as well as plain hard work. I echo poet E.E. Cummings' words, "It takes courage to grow up and turn out to be who you really are."

In my personal experience, it has been well worth the sweat and tears required. The gifts along the way are of utmost value and to be cherished. Along this journey called motherhood, I have found that which my soul sought for so long. As I dispense grace to myself and to my family, it is more accessible and can flow over and out into the world and upon each person I meet along my way. This journey began as Mark, our sons, and I dreamed of and got ready for the arrival of two beautiful girls into the Wilson family.

As we prepared to adopt our daughters, we consulted our sons about what name to give each of them. One was named after a middle school crush! Our boys had a significant role in the naming of their sisters. Each of the girls has four names that include the Chinese name that they brought with them into our family. Amidst these extra long names are the words Grace and Joy. We had absolutely no idea how prophetic the naming of our daughters would turn out to be. Today, my heart overflows with gratitude, because I can now genuinely say that I dwell in a place of much grace and tremendous joy. Despite the promises made by my earlier religion of such a dwelling place, I didn't truly abide there until recently.

A few months ago, I sat among fellow journeyers from my diverse and growing faith community. As only God can arrange through the twists and turns of life, this meeting was at the home of the therapist who worked with our family when our third grade son was in need of help for anxiety. This man was the person who first gently and kindly pointed out to me that it would be helpful to our family dynamic if I would begin to soften as a mom. With a pounding heart and tears in my eyes, I was able to publicly thank him for being the starting point for a very long journey toward parenting from a foundation of grace. I shared that as I stood on the brink of releasing my painful, hopeful, redemptive story out into the world, I was so very grateful for his words spoken to me in love over seventeen years ago.

As our group was breaking up to leave, my pastor, Lisa, came up to me and said that my story had really touched her. I looked into her face and with authenticity said to her, "I feel like I have been wandering in a wilderness for a long time. But tonight, I feel like I have found home."

On three different occasions, Mark and I brought a baby son home from the hospital to join our family. Twice, we brought a toddler daughter into our home after a twenty-four hour flight from China. In reality, becoming Mom to each of these individual and beautiful souls brought me home. It is a space filled with both external and internal freedom. It is a home full of grace and joy.

THANK YOU

There are so very many friends and family who have played meaningful roles in encouraging me to be the person that I am today. There are far too many to name, but at the top of the list, I have gratitude for these:

Thank you to my parents for loving me and for giving me the freedom and courage to pursue my voice and passions. Thank you for taking me to church and inviting me into this most interesting journey of faith.

I give a big shout out of thanks to my writing coach, Ed Cyzewski. Because of your suggestions, edits, and kind persistence, this rookie author has written a much better book. Thanks also to Mark and Liisa for your invaluable feedback. And to my son Chris, thank you for being my "web guy" and book cover designer.

Thank you to my friend Rose Lynne Clinkscales Bowman of Winston-Salem, NC who created the beautiful artwork and "storyboard" of my life that hangs in our kitchen and is partially revealed on my book cover. It truly was "a gift of love" and the product of a thirty-year friendship. I am most grateful for you.

There are quite a few mental health professionals who have played critical roles in our family's life. Thank you to David, Greta, Kim, Patti, Erin, and Beverly for guiding and challenging me along the journey toward true grace for myself, for my children, and for others. And to Eva, thank you feels a bit shallow. I have tremendous gratitude for you. I would not be living this abundant life without you.

Throughout my life I have experienced over and over the gift of friendship. Thank you to each and every one of you. In particular, thank you to Kim for always believing in me; to Martha for understanding the journey and making me laugh; to Liisa for teaching me grit, literally sweating out the material for this book, and for walking the pilgrimage alone and together; to Peggy for always being a safe, accepting place.

Thank you to my "young mom" neighbors Nicole and Yasmin. Watching you grow as mothers and sharing your children in the everyday interactions is a joy and delight. Thanks for being two of my biggest cheerleaders. And thank you Emily for being my west coast fan and for introducing me to Circle of Security International.

To each and every one of my blog readers, THANK-YOU. You have loved, challenged, and encouraged me along a five-year journey that led to this book.

Thank you to my Amazing Families fellow adoptive moms. You set my feet onto the path of this motherhood transformation. I am looking forward to our ten-year reunion.

Thank you to my Better Together sisters. You taught me to breathe in, "grace received" and breathe out, "grace released." Monthly, you encourage me to listen for God, use my voice, and speak my truth.

Thank you to my small and mighty pastor Lisa and the Southeast Raleigh Table of ESUMC. After a long time in the wilderness, it is nice to feel like I am home.

To each one of my children, thank you for being you and challenging me to be the best that I can be. It is a joy, honor, and delight to watch you grow and become your own special self. You are the grace bearers in my life. I love you from the depths of my being.

And to Mark, my husband and best friend, I love and choose you. Thank you for loving and choosing me. What a journey! I look forward to growing old alongside you.

The Wilson clan 2017

Dear Reader,

I invite you to connect with me at tricia-wilson.com. There is a monthly newsletter subscription option as well as a way to follow blog posts and interact with each other. If you are feeling generous and kind, please consider reviewing this book on Amazon. Thank you for coming along on this journey.

Adopt grace,
Tricia

BOOK SUGGESTIONS

There are so many great ones out there, but this is a list that I have used along my journey. The reading of books has played a huge role in both my faith and parenting shifts. Here are a few of my favorites in various categories related to the themes and messages in this book.

Matters of Faith

Any and all books by these authors, in no particular order: Anne Lamott, Richard Rohr, Wendell Berry, Glennon Doyle Melton, Kent Annan, Phillip Yancey, Shane Claiborne, Lauren Winner, Richard Foster, Ann Voskamp, Brennan Manning, Sarah Bessey, Kathleen Norris, Joan Chittister, Rowan Williams, Henri Nouwen, Paula D'Arcy, Walter Brueggemann, Jim Wallis, Gregory Boyle, Tony Campolo, Eugene Peterson, Lewis B. Smedes, John A. Sanford, John O'Donohue, Thomas Merton, Adam Hamilton (especially *Making Sense of the Bible: Rediscovering the Power of Scripture Today*)

Matters of Psychology and Living as a Whole Person

Books by Brené Brown, Harriet Lerner, M. Scott Peck
Boundaries by Dr. Henry Cloud and Dr. John Townsend

General Parenting and Development

Conscious Discipline (workbook) by Dr. Becky A. Bailey

What Am I Feeling? By Dr.John Gottman and Talaris Research Institute

The Whole Brain Child by Dr.Daniel Siegel and Dr. Tina Payne Bryson

Parenting from the Inside Out by Dr. Daniel Siegel and Mary Hartzell

Any book that has Dr. Daniel Siegel as an author or co-author

How To Talk So Kids Will Listen & Listen So Kids Will Talk by Adele Faber and Elaine Mazlish

Raising Your Spirited Child and *Kids, Parents, and Power Struggles* by Mary Sheedy Kurcinka

Parenting for Peace by Dr. Marcy Axness

Play: How It Shapes the Brain, Opens the Imagination, and Invigorates the Soul by Dr. Stuart Brown with Christopher Vaughn

Parenting Adolescents and Teens

Untangled by Dr. Lisa Damour

Mothering and Daughtering by Sil and Eliza Reynolds

The Mother-Daughter Project by Dr. SuEllen Hamkins and Renée Schultz

Hold Onto Your Kids: Why Parents Need to Matter More Than Peers by Dr. Gordon Neufeld and Dr. Gabor Maté

Queen Bees and Wannabes by Rosalind Wiseman

Girls & Sex: Navigating the Complicated New Landscape by Peggy Orenstein

Attachment resources

Circle of Security, International

Theraplay: Helping Parents and Children Build Better Relationships Through Attachment-Based Play by Ann M. Jernberg and Phyllis B. Booth

Regarding Adult Attachment Issues: *Attachments: Why You Love, Feel and Act the Way You Do* by Dr. Tim Clinton and Dr. Gary Sibcy

Adoption Specific Resources

The Connected Child by Dr. Karyn Purvis and Dr. David Cross, and Wendy Lyons Sunshine

Attaching in Adoption by Deborah D. Gray

Parenting Your Internationally Adopted Child by Patty Cogen

Twenty Things Adopted Kids Wish Their Adoptive Parents Knew by Sherrie Eldridge

20 Things Adoptive Parents Need to Succeed by Sherrie Eldridge

Talking with Young Children about Adoption by Mary Watkins and Susan Fisher

Lifebooks: Creating a Treasure for the Adopted Child by Beth O'Malley

Conferences sponsored by Empowered to Connect

Parenting Children with Trauma or Other Special Needs

Far From the Tree: Parents, Children, and the Search for Identity by Andrew Solomon

Adopting the Hurt Child by Dr. Gregory C.Keck and Regina M. Kupecky

Wounded Children Healing Homes by Jayne E. Schooler, Betsy Keefer Smalley, and Dr. Timothy Callahan

The Body Keeps the Score by Dr. Bessel van der Kolk

From Fear to Love by B. Bryan Post

Beyond Consequences, Logic, and Control by Heather T. Forbes and B. Bryan Post

The Great Behavior Breakdown by B. Bryan Post

The Out of Sync Child and *The Out of Sync Child Has Fun* by Carol Stock Kranowitz

The Chemistry of Connection by Susan Kuchinskas

Chinese Adoption Specific

Wanting a Daughter, Needing a Son and *China's Hidden Children* by Kay Ann Johnson

From Home to Homeland: What Adoptive Families Need to Know before Making a Return Trip to China edited by Debra Jacobs, Iris Chin Ponte, and Leslie Kim Wang

Works of Fiction

These are too numerous to name, but I love reading authors who are somehow "other." Whether it be race, experience, sexual orientation, religion, etc., etc., etc., these are my favorites. I learn so much by listening to the voices of others.

END NOTES

1 Proverbs 19:21, New International Version

2 Michael D. Marlowe, "The Chicago Statement on Biblical Inerrancy," http://www.bible-researcher.com/chicago1.html

3 Anne Marie and Gary Ezzo, *Growing Kids God's Way: Reaching the Heart of Your Child With a God-Centered Purpose*, 1997.

4 Tim Kimmel, *Grace Based Parenting*, 2005.

5 Dr. Karyn Purvis, Empowered to Connect Conference, Orlando, FL, February 15-16, 2013.

6 Francis of Assisi paraphrased by Daniel Ladinsky, *Love Poems from God: Twelve Voices from the East and West* (Penguin Compass: 2002), p. 37.

7 Charlie Custer, http://www.theatlantic.com/china/archive/2013/07/kidnapped-and-sold-inside-the-dark-world-of-child-trafficking-in-china/278107/ Sushma Subramanian and Deborah Jian Lee http://www.theatlantic.com/international/archive/2011/10/black-market-babies-broken-families-in-china-confused-children-in-the-us/247329/ Mirah Riben http://www.huffingtonpost.com/mirah-riben/adoption-crimes-and-corru_b_6467540.html David Smolin, Samford University, https://works.bepress.com/david_smolin, Kay Ann Johnson, *China's Hidden Children* (Chicago, The University of Chicago Press, 2016)

8 Liz Latty, "What We Lost: Undoing the Fairy Tale Narrative of Adoption," The Rumpus, November 17, 2016.

9 Anne Lamott, "The Jesuit Rec Room with Anne Lamott," August 24, 2015, www.youtube.com/watch?v=iMoJdTVSyzY

10 Parker J. Palmer, *Let Your Life Speak: Listening for the Voice of Vocation*, (San Francisco, Jossey-Bass, 2000)

11 http://www.dictionary.com/browse/scapegoat?s=t

12 *The Book of Common Prayer*, (New York: Church Publishing, 1979), p. 22.

13 I John 4:18, New International Version.

[14]Elizabeth O'Brien, M.A. "Mirroring," September 10, 2011, http://www.elizobrien.com/mirroring/.

[15] David Seamands, *Healing for Damaged Emotions* (Colorado Springs, David C. Cook, 2015), p. 83.

[16] Dr. Tim Clinton and Dr. Gary Sibcy, *Attachments: Why You Love, Feel, and Act the Way You Do* (Brentwood: Thomas Nelson Publishers, 2002),p. 131-144.

See Daniel Siegel, *The Developing Mind: How Relationships and the Brain Interact to Shape Who We Are* (New York: The Guilford Press, 2012)

Kent Hoffman, Circle of Security Parenting Training, April 25-28, 2017, Cary, North Carolina.

[17] John 8:32, New International Version

[18] John Gottman, Ph.D. and Talaris Research Institute, *What Am I Feeling?* (Seattle, Parenting Press, Inc., 2004), p. 9-25.

[19] Ibid., p. 13.

[20] Brene´ Brown, *Daring Greatly* (New York: Penguin Group, 2012), p. 214-245.

[21] Ibid, pg. 238.

[22] Sil Reynolds, RN and Eliza Reynolds, *Mothering and Daughtering: Keeping Your Bond Strong Through the Teen Years* (Boulder: Sounds True, Inc., 2013), p. 58.

[23] Isaiah 55:8, New International Version

[24] Brené Brown, Ph.D., L.M.S.W.*The Gifts of Imperfection: Let Go of Who You Think You're Supposed to Be and Embrace Who You Are* (Center City, Hazelden, 2010), p. 72-73.

[25] Dr. Becky Bailey, *Conscious Discipline*, (Orlando, Loving Guidance, Inc., 2000), p. 157-180.

[26] Ibid, p. 162

[27] Kent Annan, *Slow Kingdom Coming* (Downers Grove, Intervarsity Press, 2016), p.120

CPSIA information can be obtained
at www.ICGtesting.com
Printed in the USA
LVOW10s1127170917
549032LV00010B/675/P